AF305183

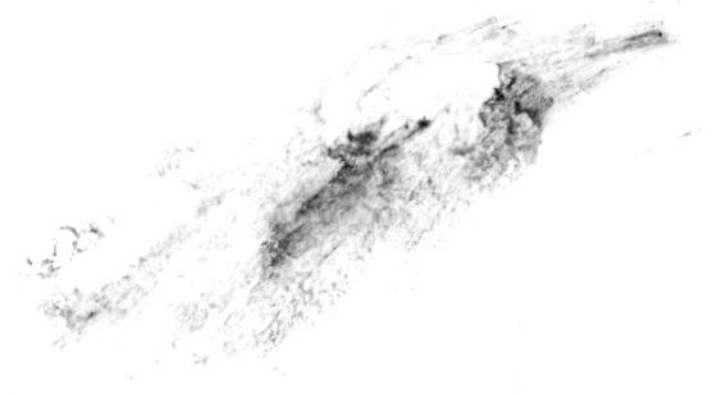

Melissa Moore   LAND ENDS

Were the earth smooth, our brains would be smooth as well;
we would wake, blink, walk two steps to get the whole picture,
and lapse into a dreamless sleep.

Annie Dillard, *Pilgrim at Tinker Creek*

Melissa Moore

LAND ENDS

SKIRA

Cover
Talisman

Design
Marcello Francone

Editorial Coordination
Emma Cavazzini

Special Editor
Filippo Maggia

Editing
Anna Albano

Layout
Anna Cattaneo

First published in Italy in 2013 by
Skira Editore S.p.A.
Palazzo Casati Stampa
via Torino 61
20123 Milano
Italy
www.skira.net

Printed and bound in Italy. First edition

ISBN: 978-88-572-1939-4

Distributed by Thames and Hudson Ltd., 181A High
Holborn, London WC1V 7QX, United Kingdom.

Acknowledgements, Special Thanks

Filippo Maggia
Stefano Piantini

Mark Cousins
Douglas Park
Persilia Caton

Marcella Mannion – Metronom

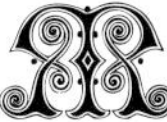

METRONOM
Olivier Richon
Rut Blees Luxemburg
Christoph Tannert - Künstlerhaus
Bethanien
David Drake
Lisa Botos - Botos Projects
Regina Anzenberger – Anzenberger
Gallery
Takeki Sugiyama - Theory of Clouds
Hilary Koob Sassen
Paul Caffell
Max Caffell
Emma Roach
Tomas Miller
Pavel Büchler
Fiona Minors
Steffi Klenz

Exceptional Gratitude

Diane Smith
Quana Parker
www.quana.net
Leia and Michael Parker
Also all my island friends including
Lloyd House
Joanne Ovistland
www.realhornby.com
Michelle St.Pierre
www.deerheartsanctuary.com/
Michael McNamera, Blue Sky Design
Brian and Judy
Bob Cain
Margaret Rabina
Tim Biggins
Angela Muellers
In memory of John Bottomley
www.johnbottomley.net
and in memory of my mother
and my father

LAND ENDS

Melissa Moore

LAND ENDS

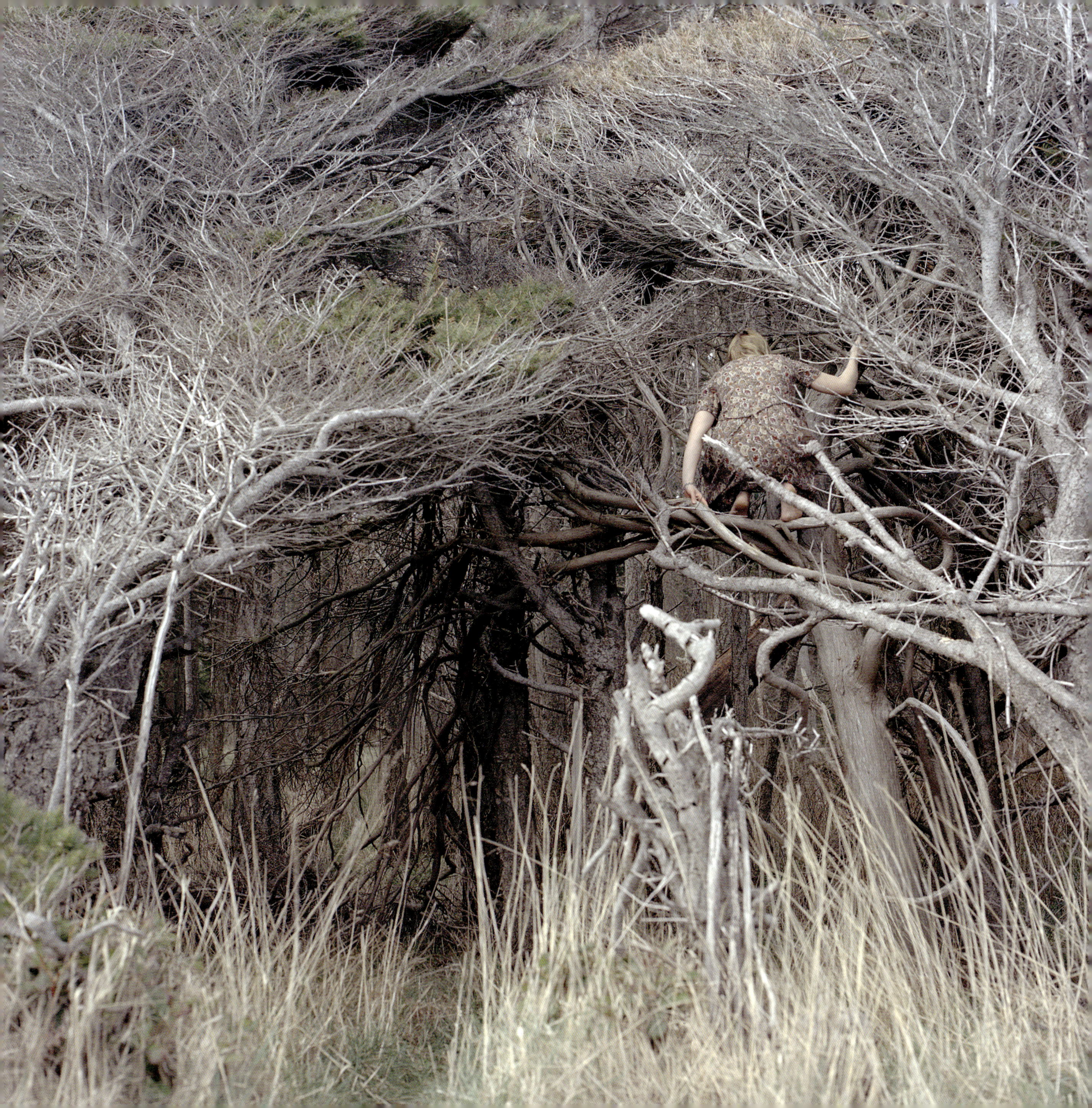

Douglas Park

STANDSTILL VOYAGE-OF-DISCOVERY ON-THE-SPOT

Compressed portable foldout bijou continent.

Cause, origins, source, genesis?

Lightweight floating ballast elephant's graveyard, stowaway mutineers, born & bred thrown overboard, lost, buried, all-at-sea.

Lifesaver deathtrap coastguard decoy awaits.

Namely, driftwood attractive magnetic adhesive glue absorbent sponge. Target, luring many times over much more of the very same, to join what's already there, as extra contributory additions. Contraband freight cargo, washed ashore, crash landing, high & dry, stranded.

Upon delivery and arrival, anchor cast, mooring found, roots lain, foundations planted. There follows widespread growth, breeding, multiplication and takeover. Alpine rockery and topiary bonsai jungle mutually fuel and reinforce each other.

Assembly-kit form self-build scheme enacts instruction-manual. Unused offcast spare-ribs basket-woven into ramshackle and makeshift clinker-built shipwreck liferaft chalet settlement.

Log-cabin flameproof bonfire. Spun cable links everywhere together. Constant tightrope catwalk suspension-bridge. Stepladder staircase.

Implant armature. Exo-skeleton scaffolding. Dry-stone wall. Stepping-stones. Balancing-act.

Somehow or other, belonging and function simply happens, where and how ever they were always destined to end up, as much component units alone by themselves, as members of vast complex mass. Any single spare-part moved away or taken out forces all the rest to collapse, domino-topple and chain-react. Shifting just 1 fixture shall pull and knock the others out of place; the entire lot, dislodged and fallen apart.

Mortis, hinge multiple-jointed marionette puppet doll population become the outpatient and resident inmate menagerie and crew that nest and blossom on and around tree-house and roof-garden built-up afforestation and overgrown settlement. Penthouse suites face the view of all below them, underneath as well, then far beyond from there.

Window-box convoy pack armada herd squadron swarm parade flock team shoal regimentally patrols along carnival-float balcony veranda terrace.

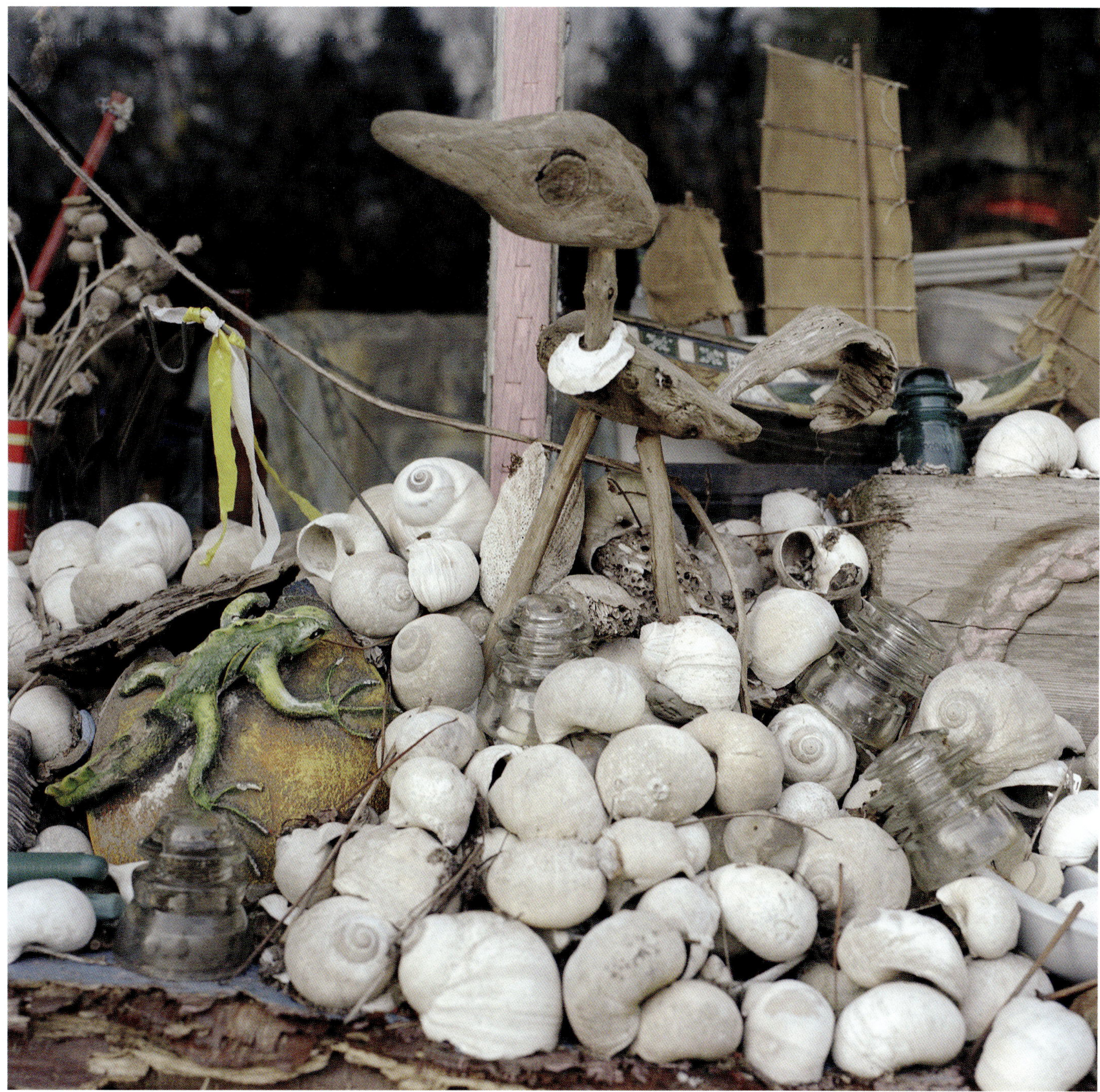

Island

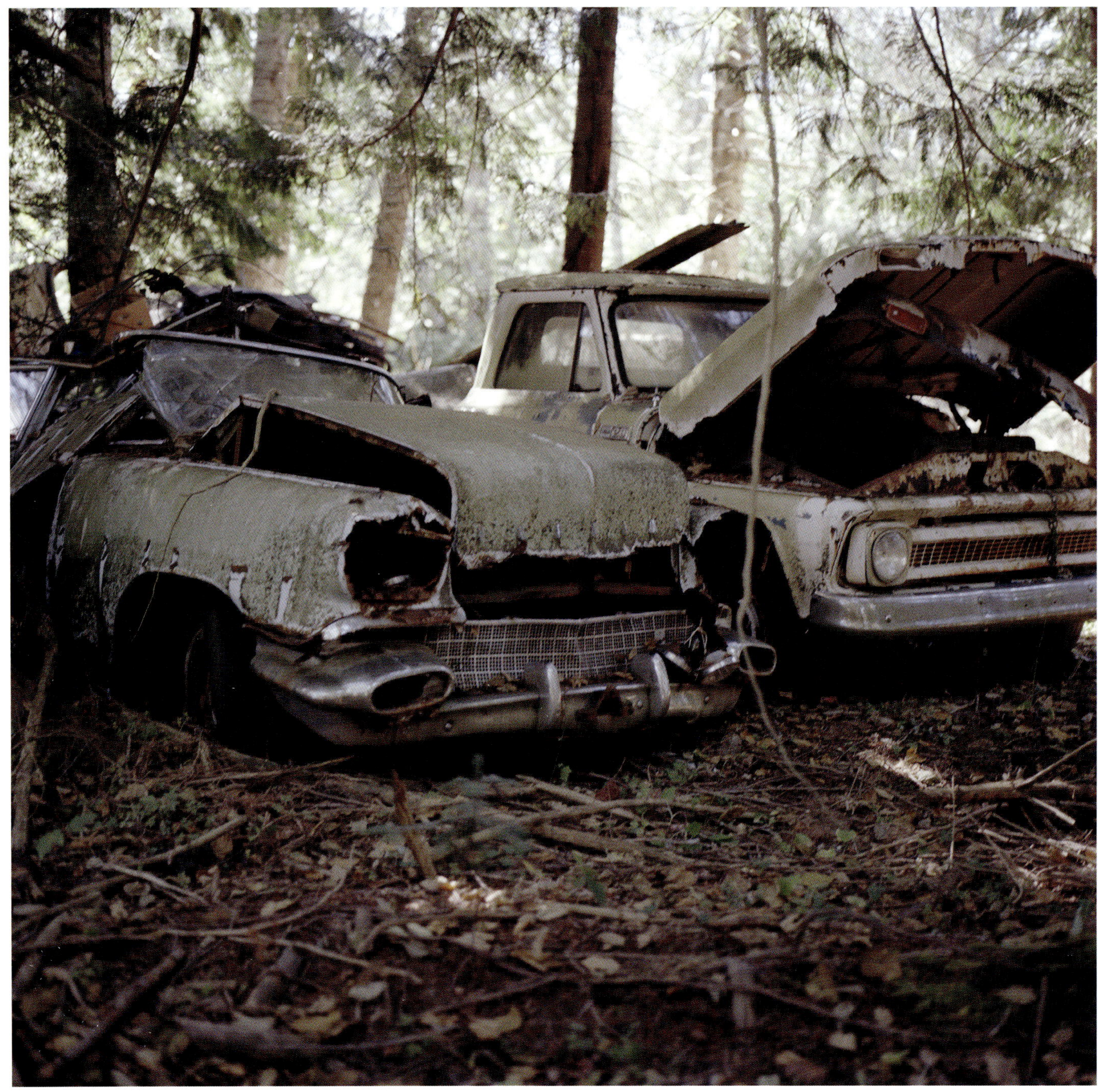

Settlement

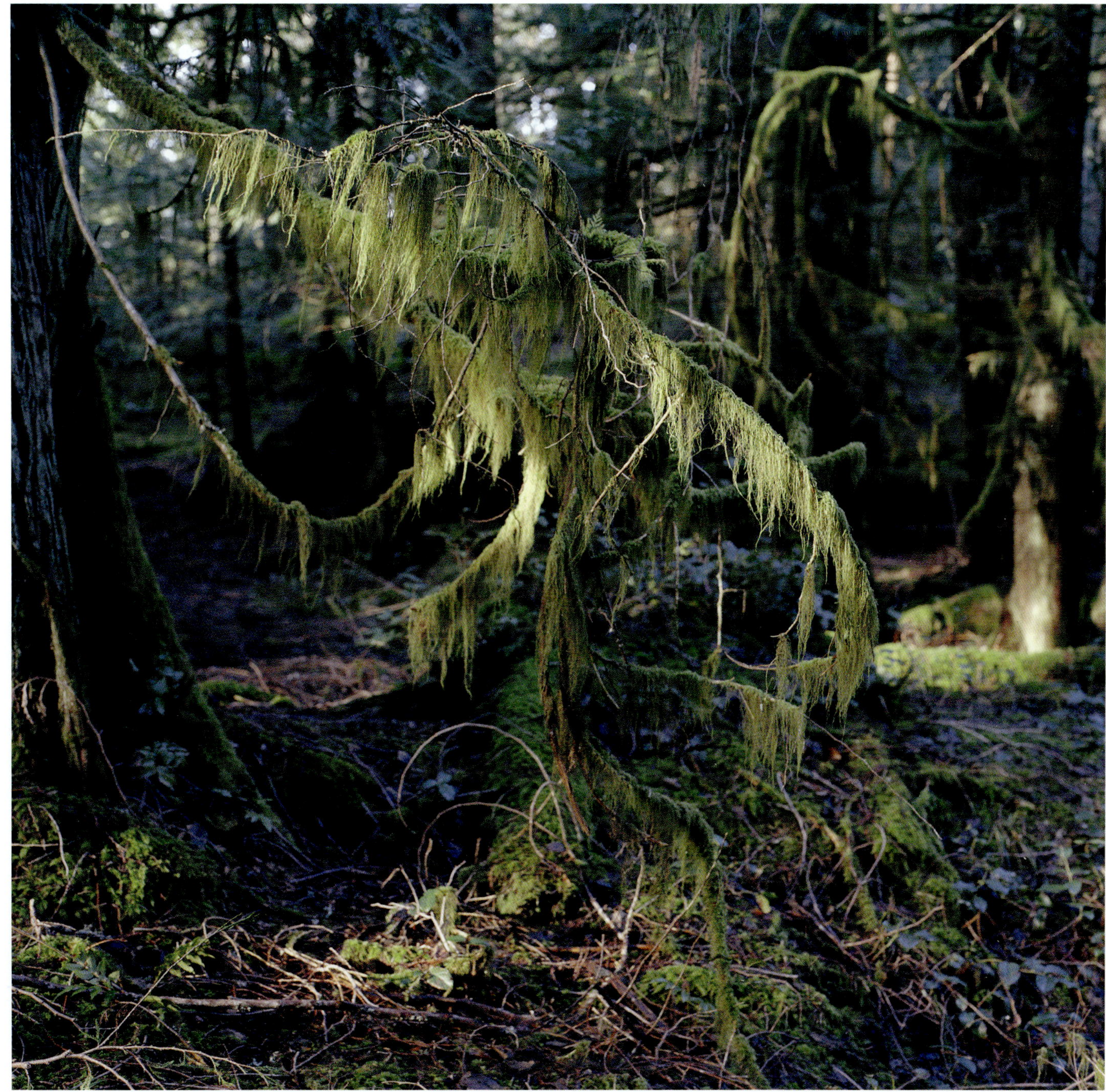

Lights

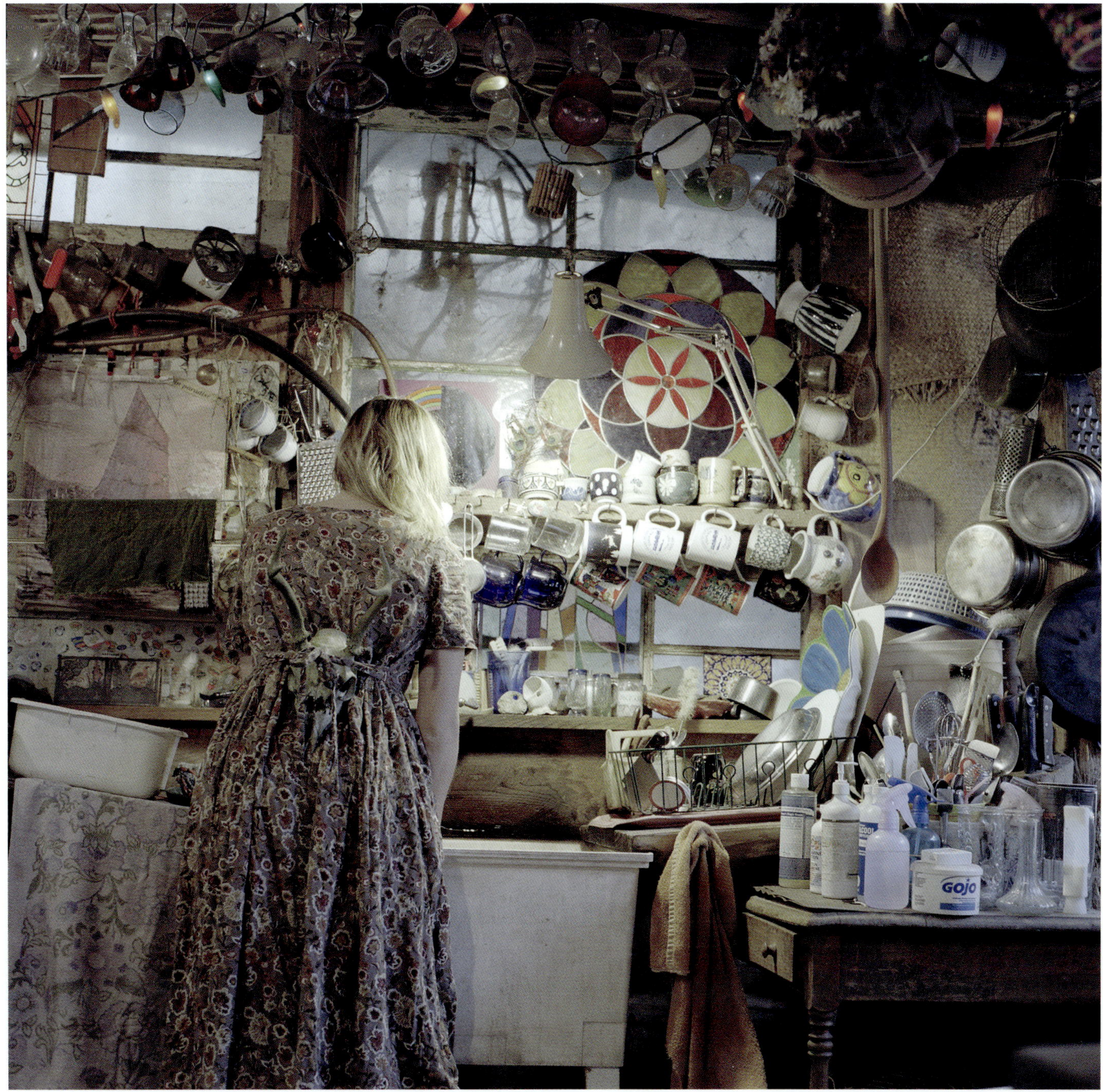

Talisman

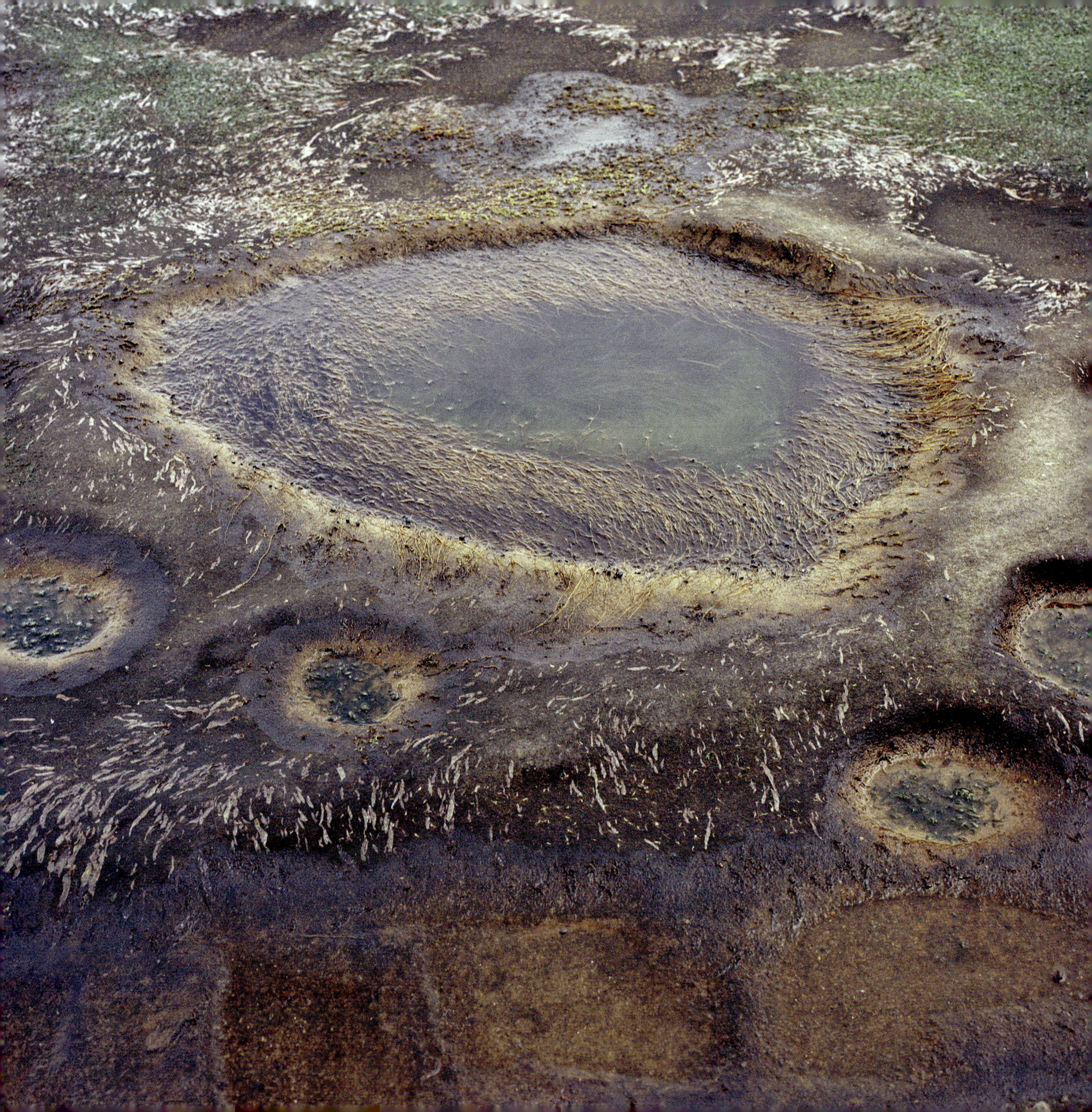

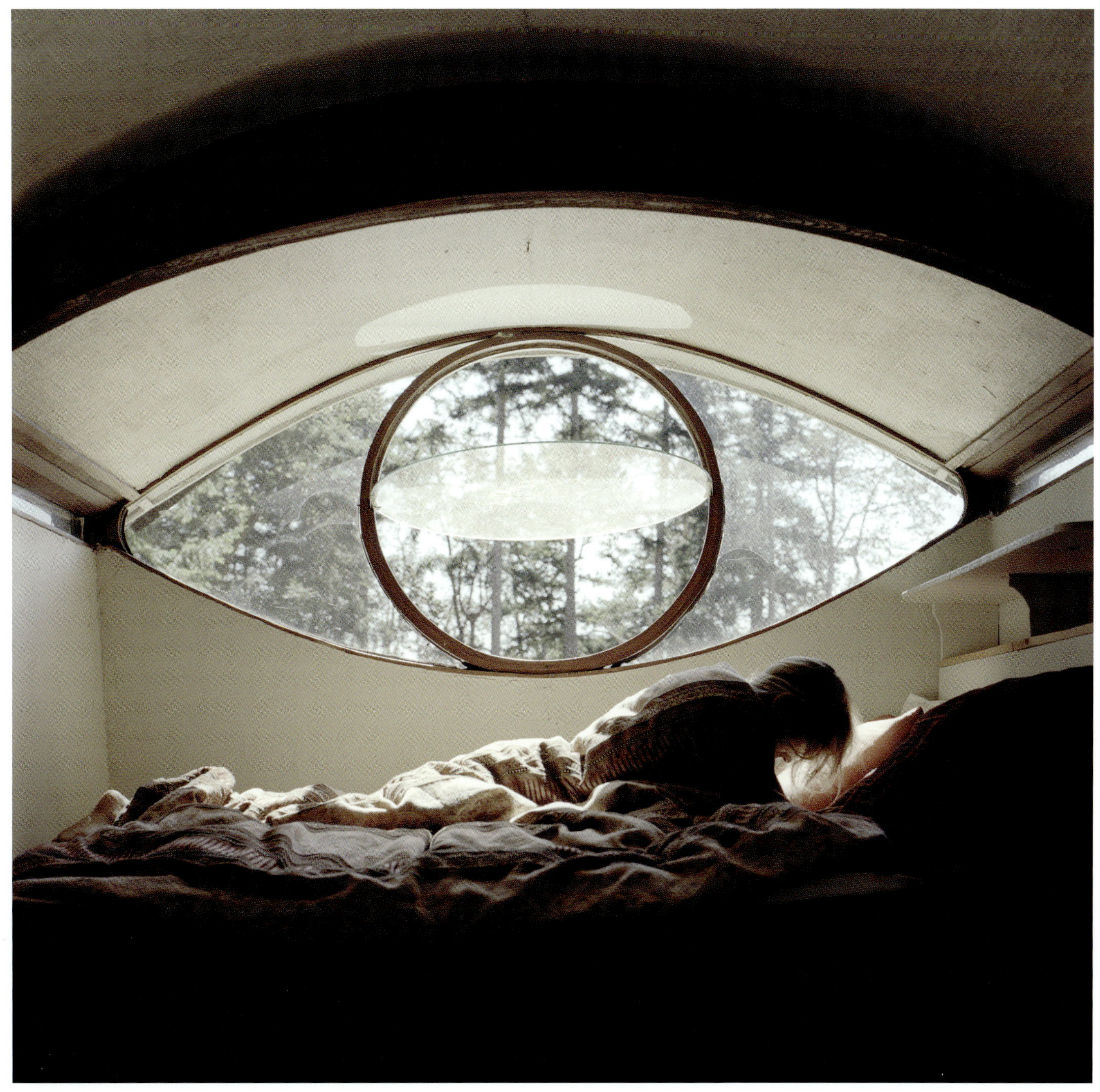

Lloyd House

Fable (Whaling Station) ▸

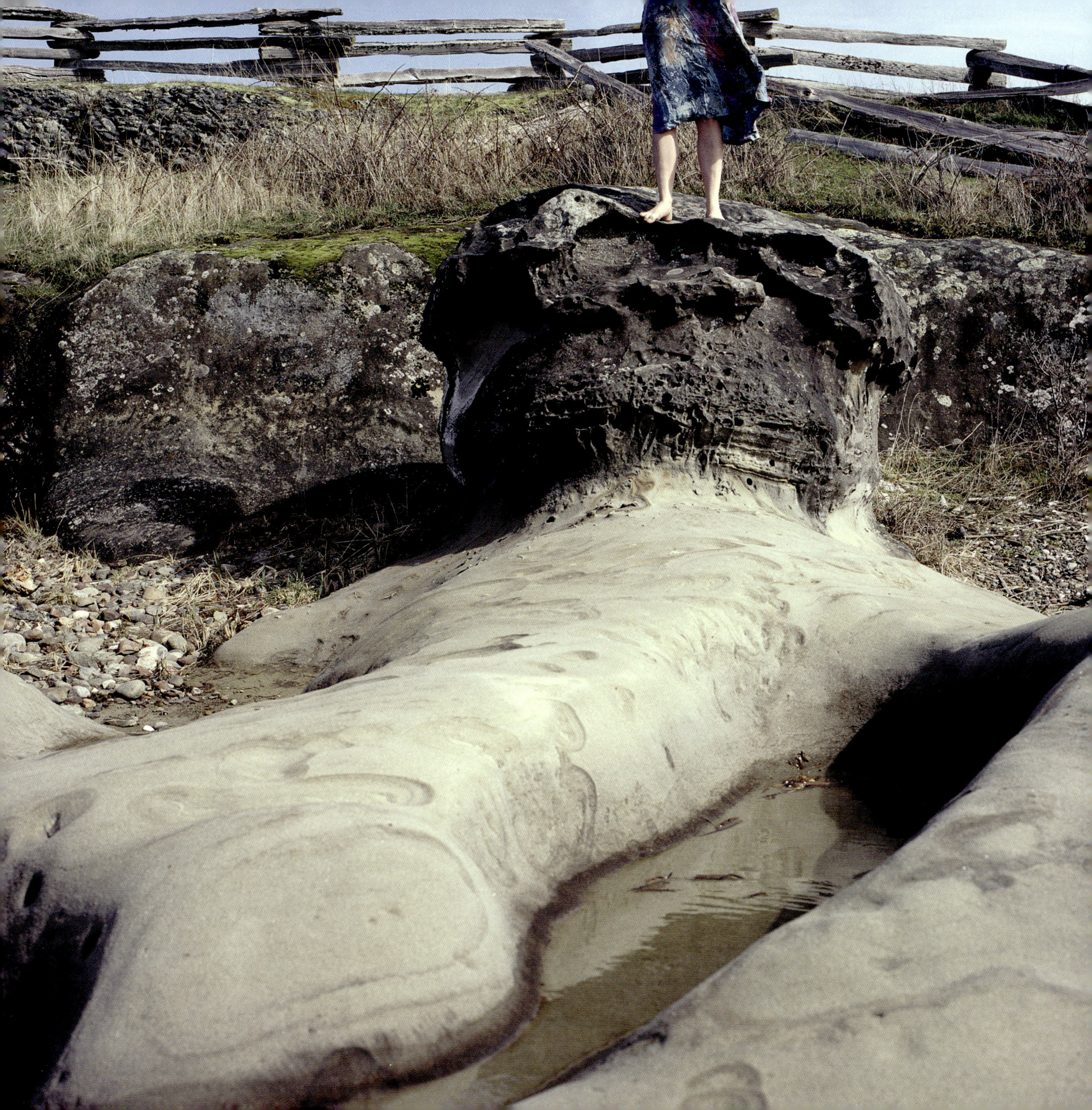

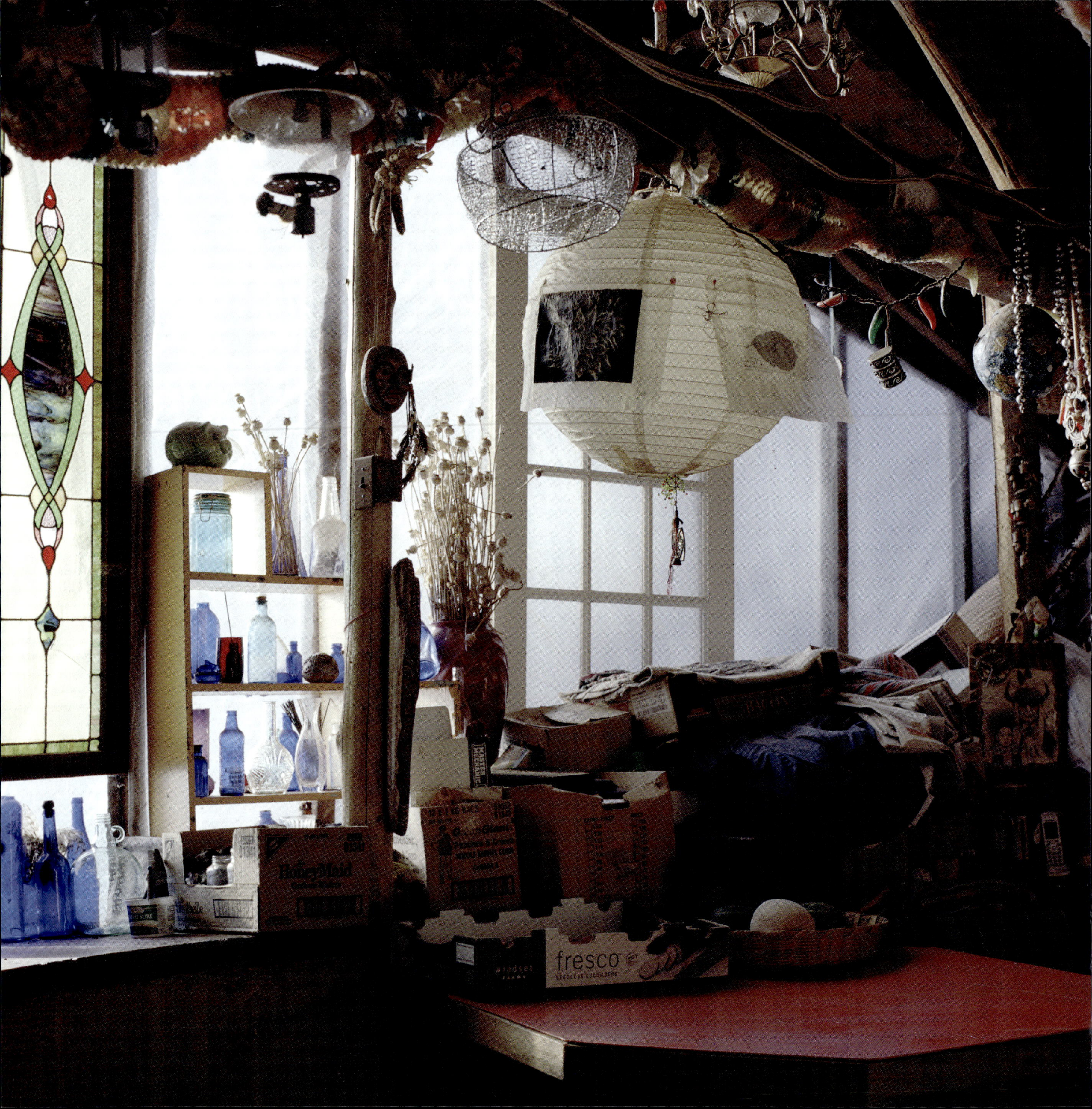

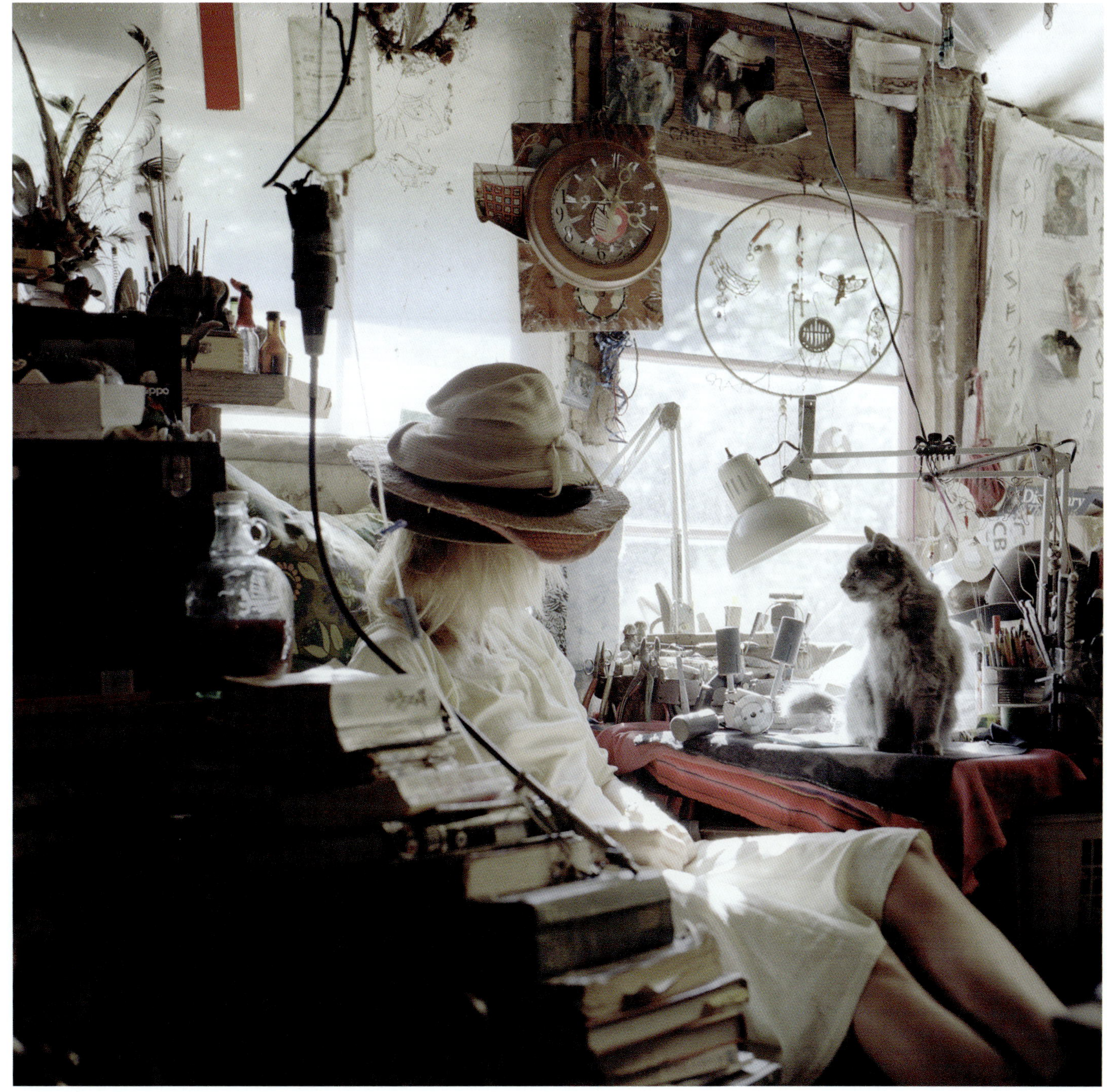

Tarot

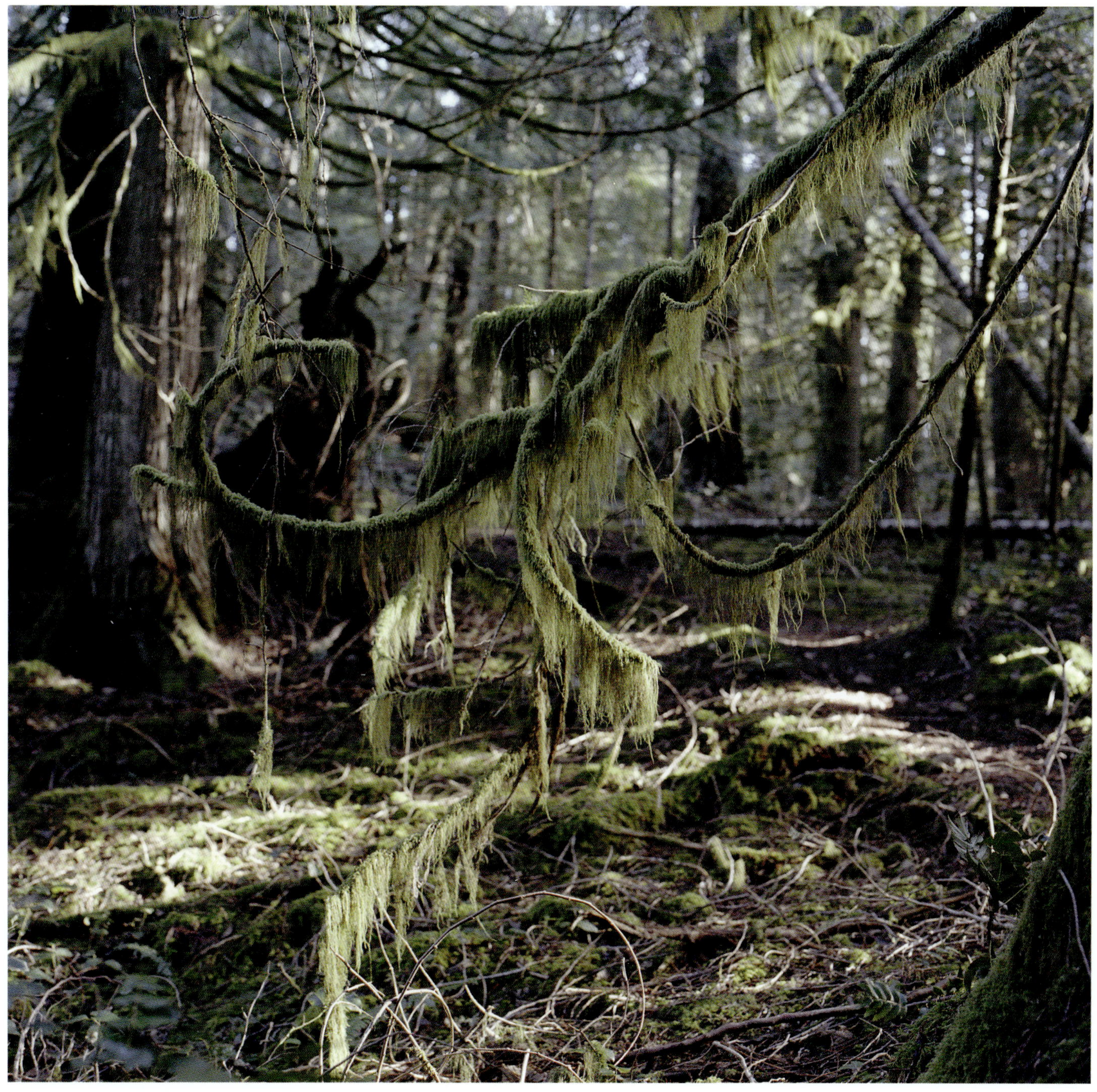

Glyph

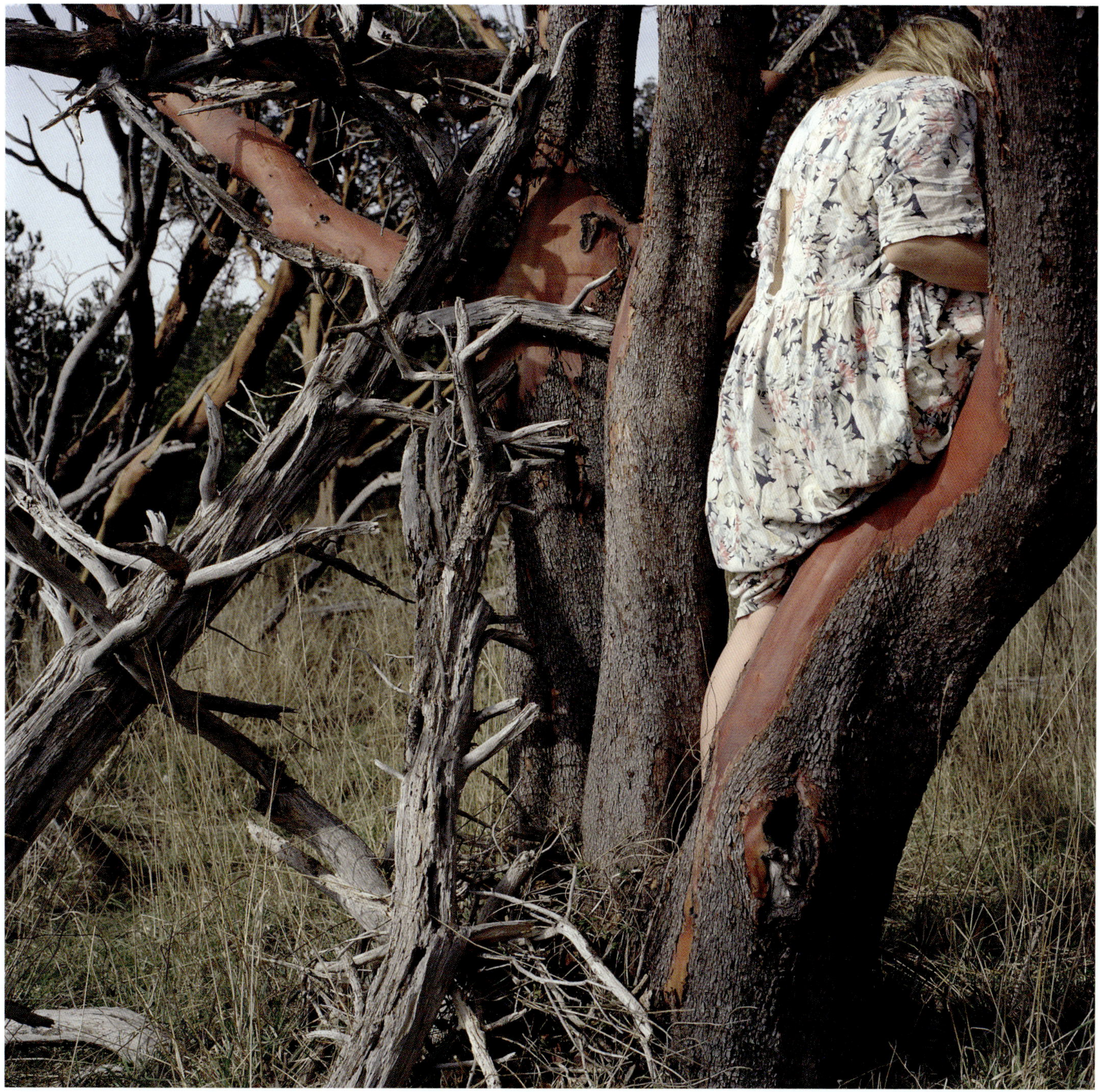

Arbutus

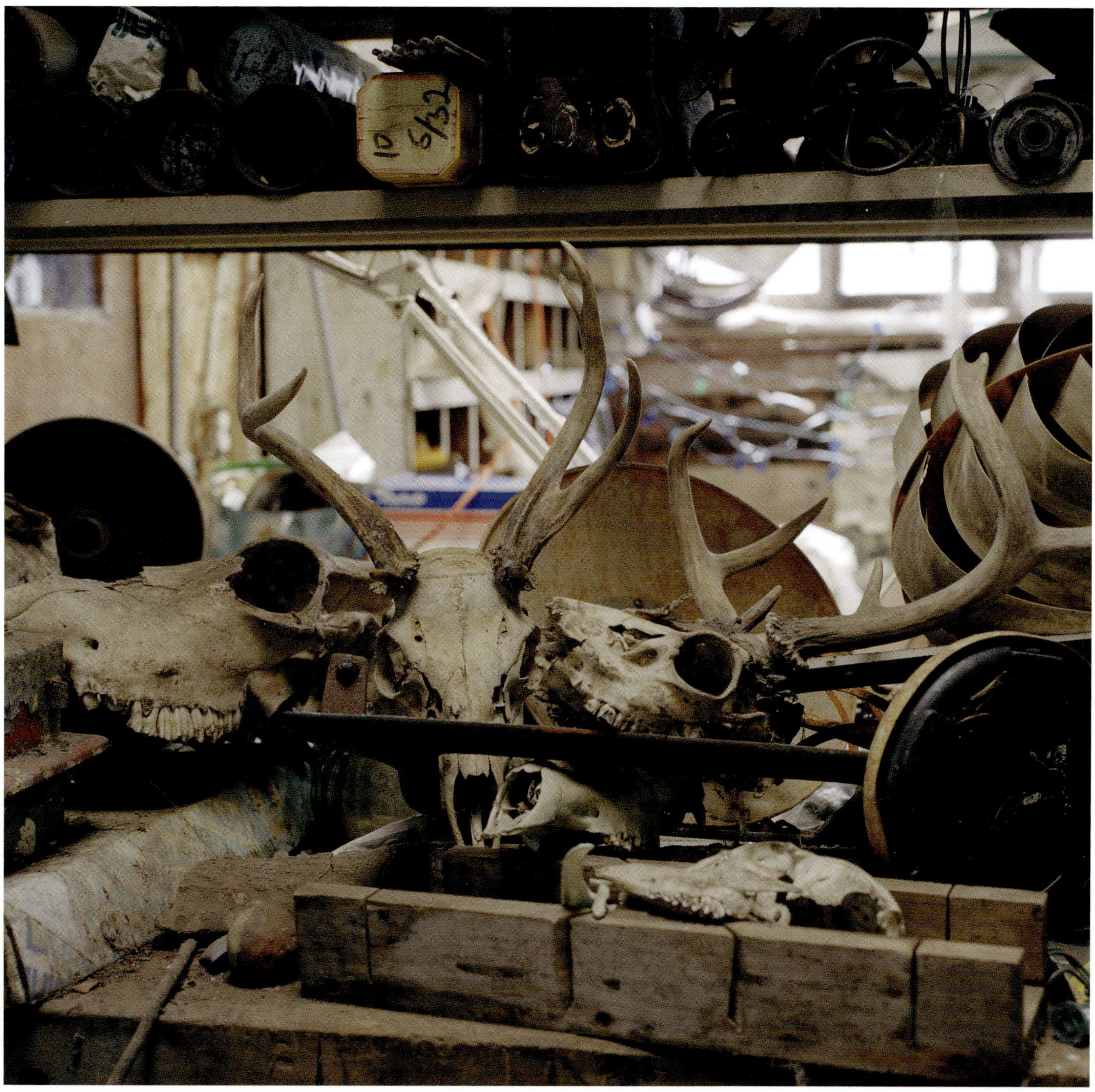

Compilation

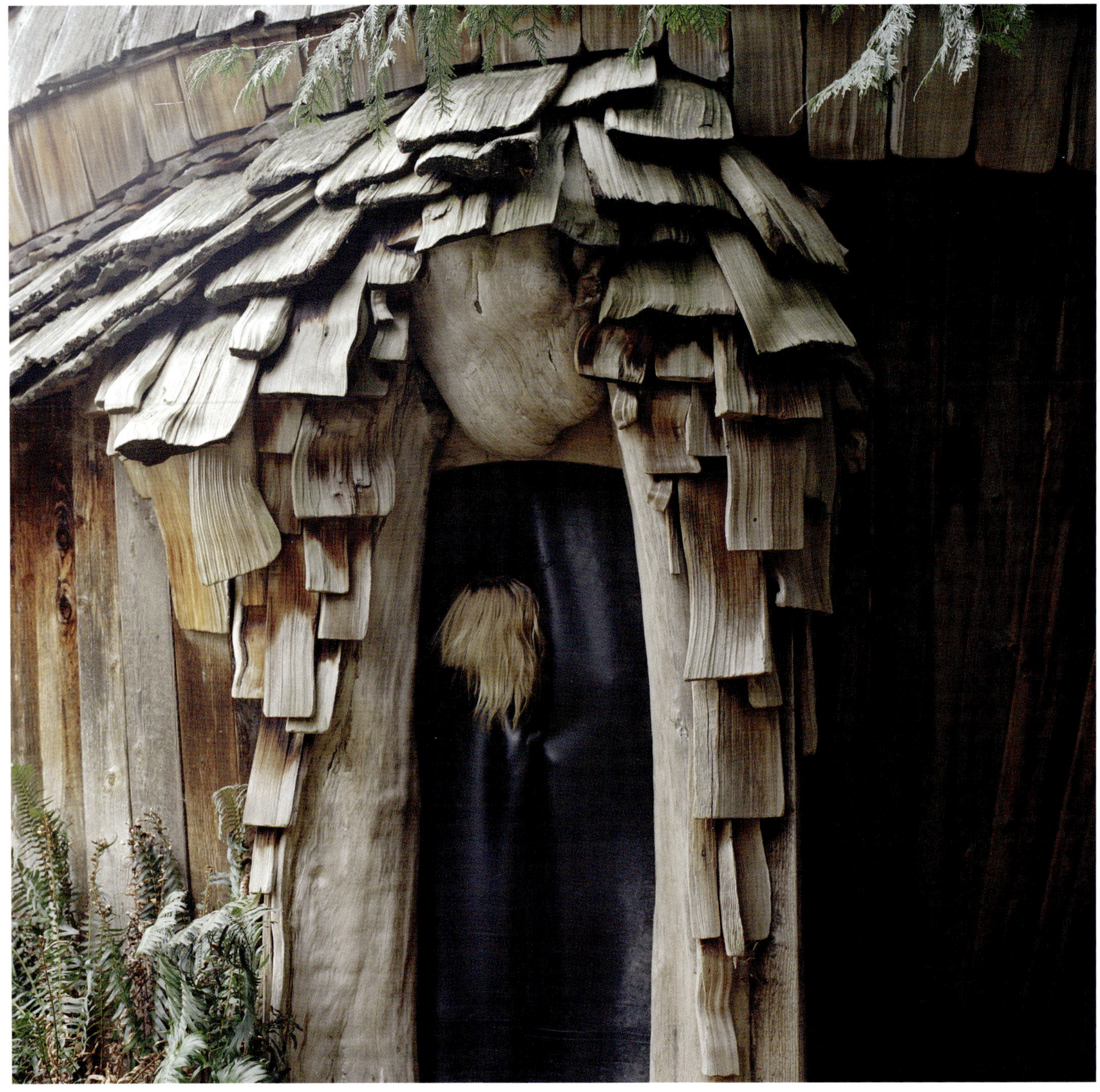

Cosmos

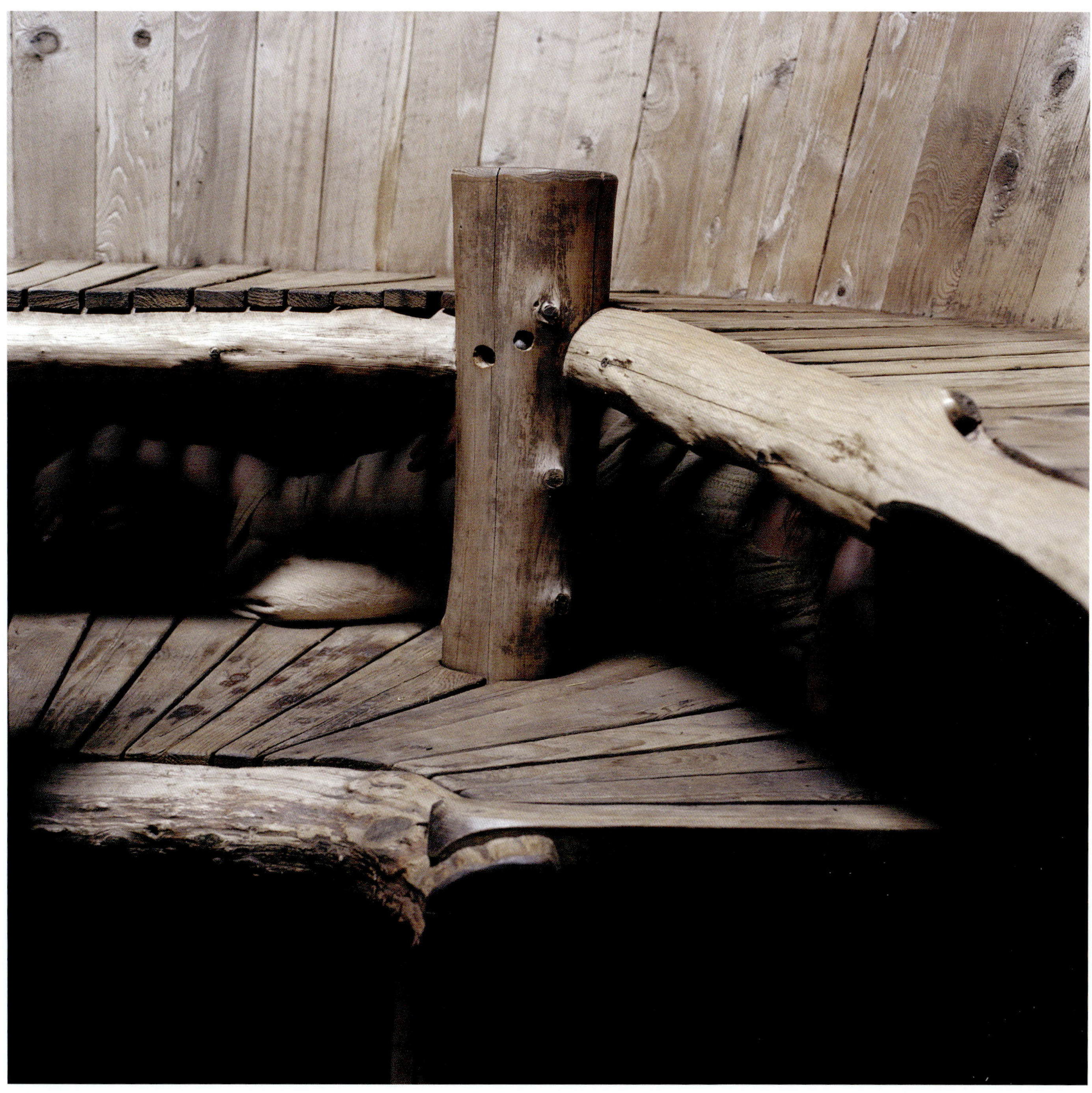

Occupation

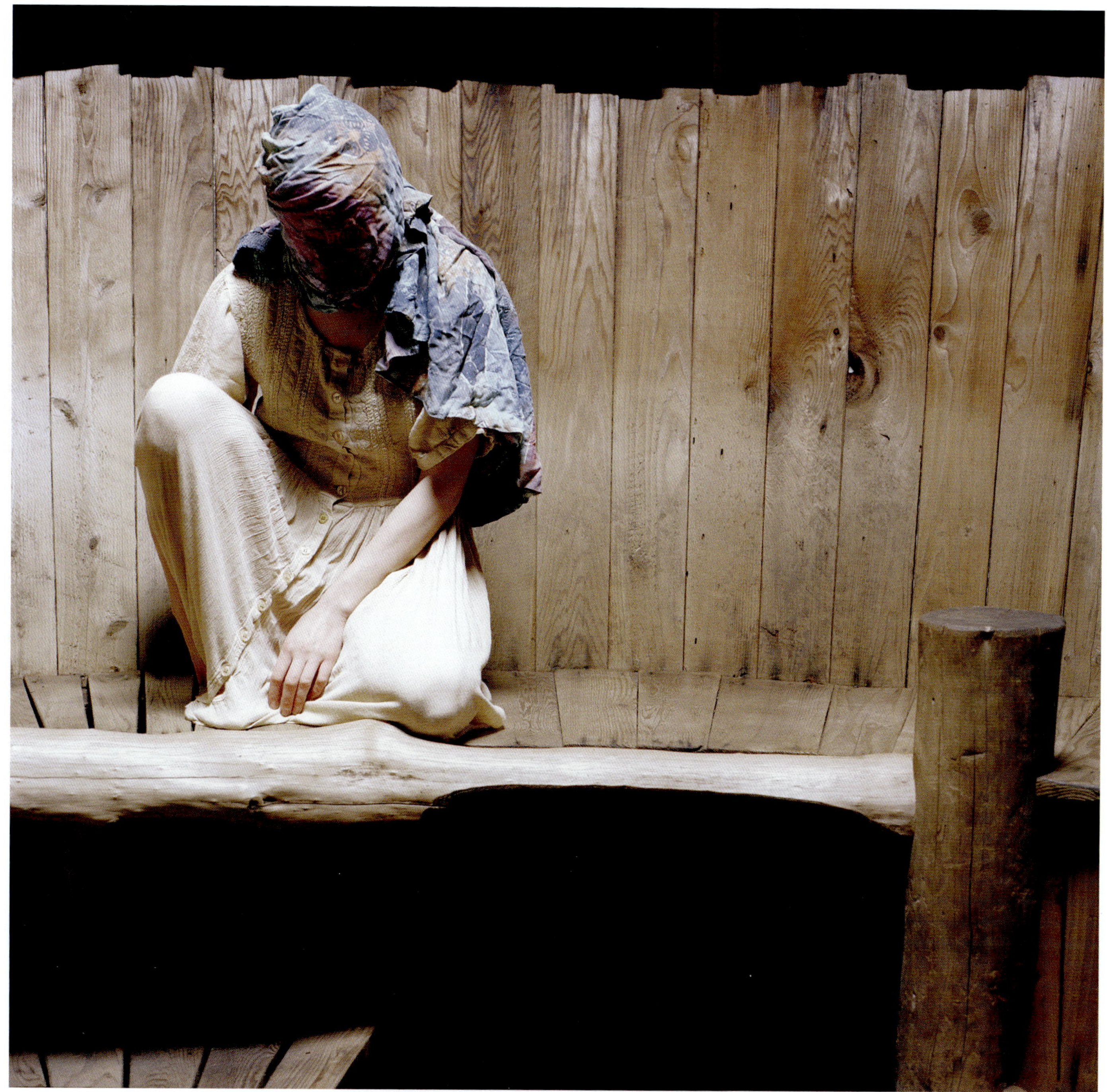

Shade

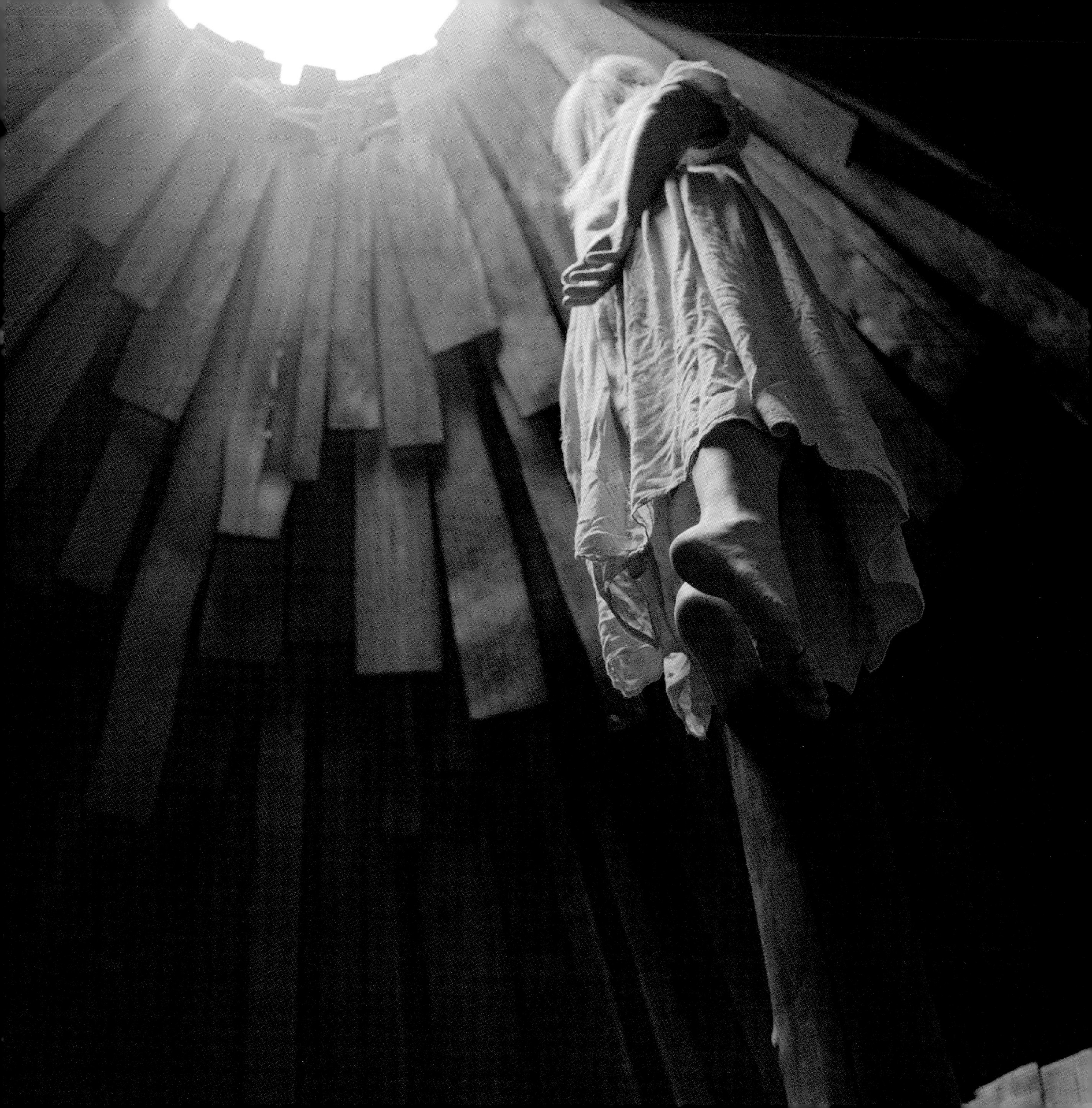

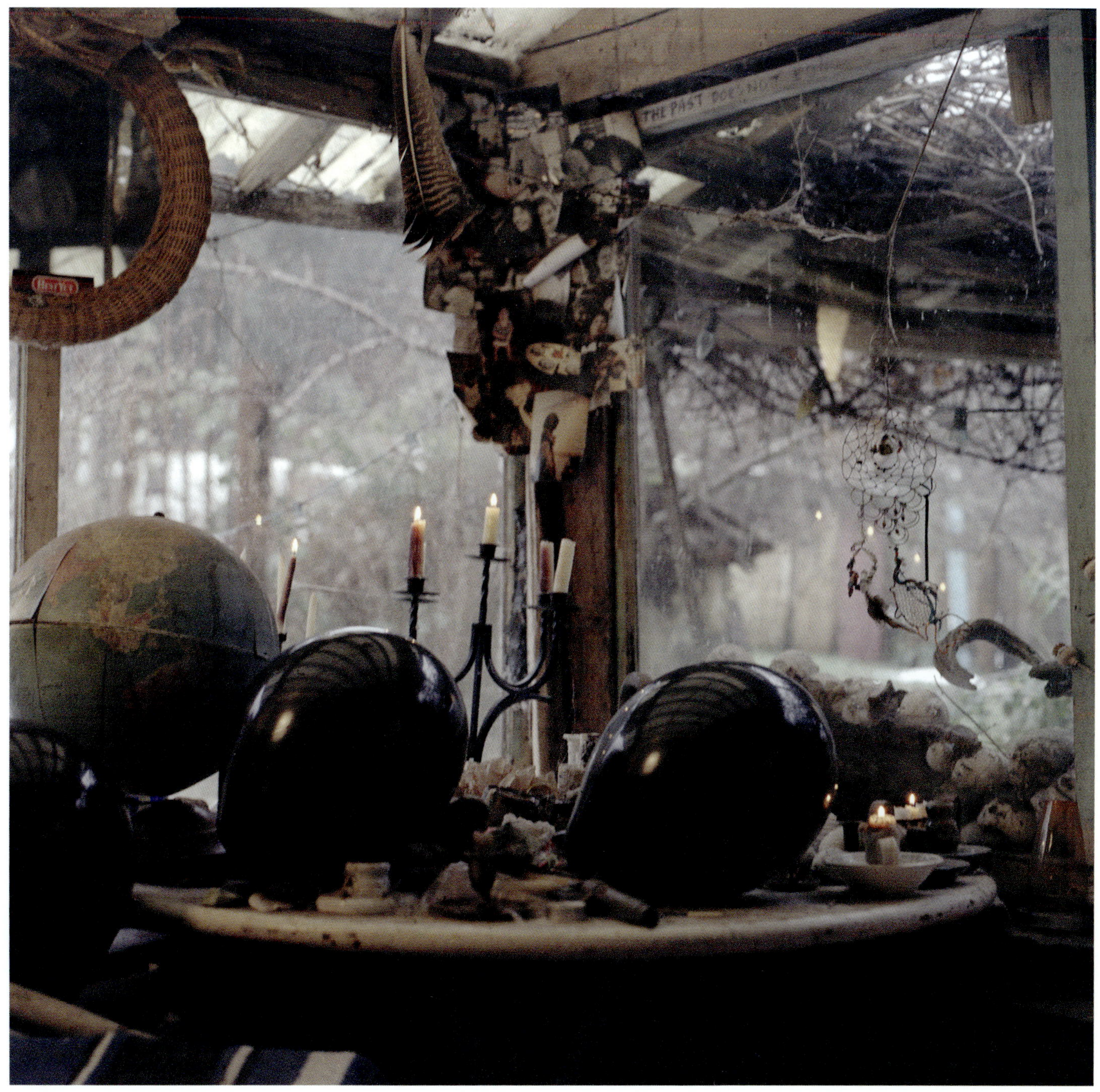

The Past

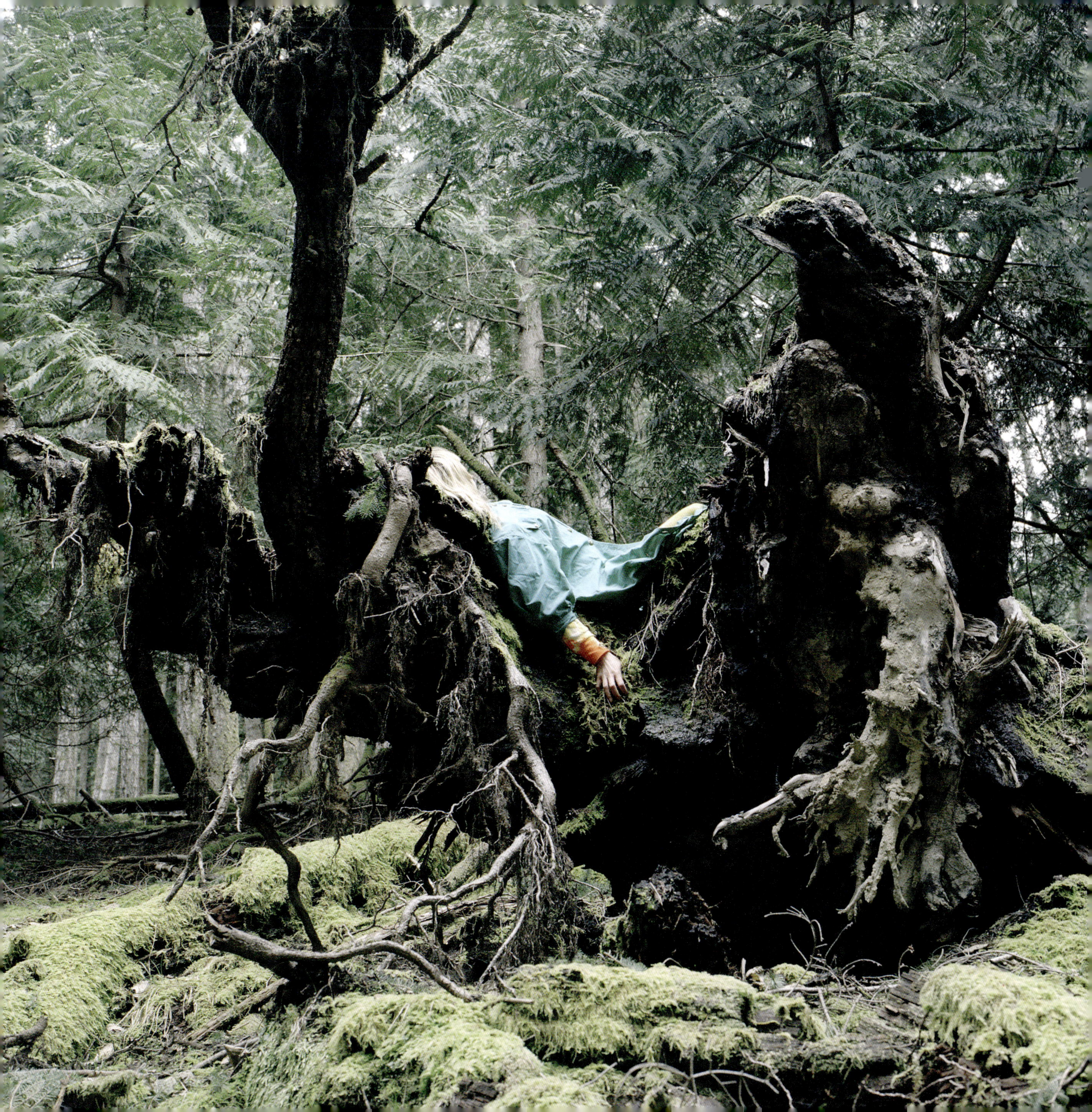

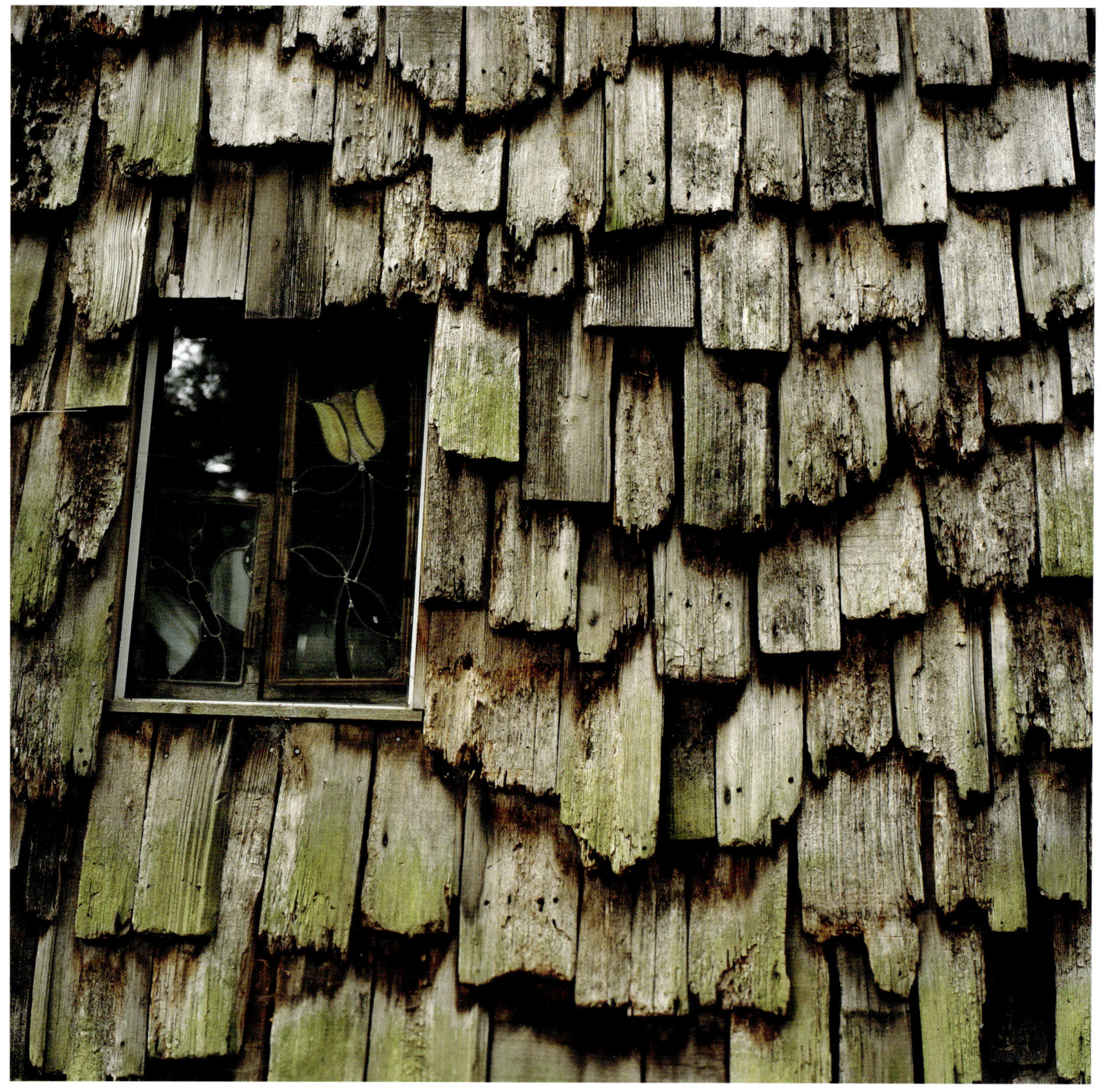

Abracadabra

Knot ▸

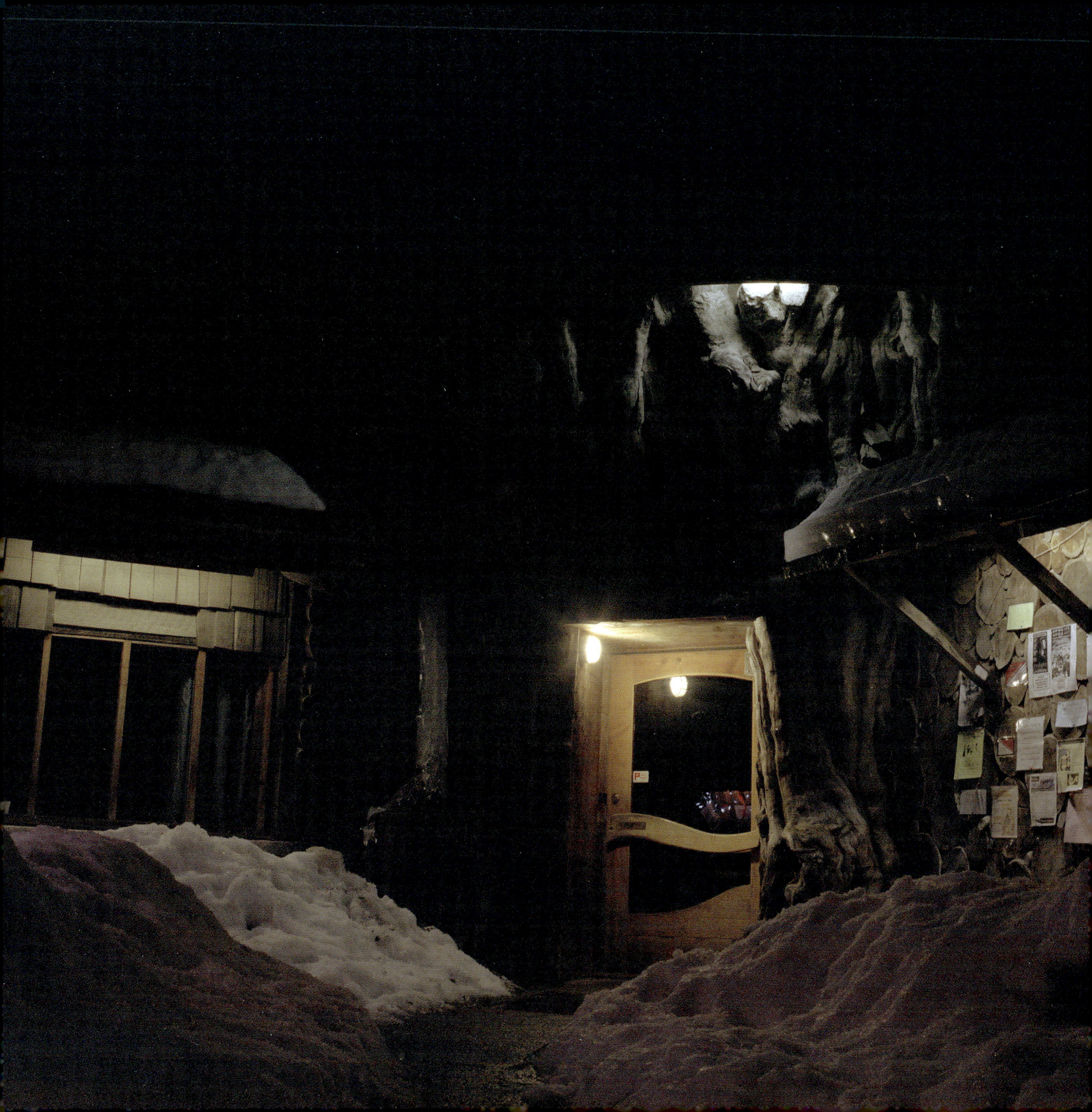

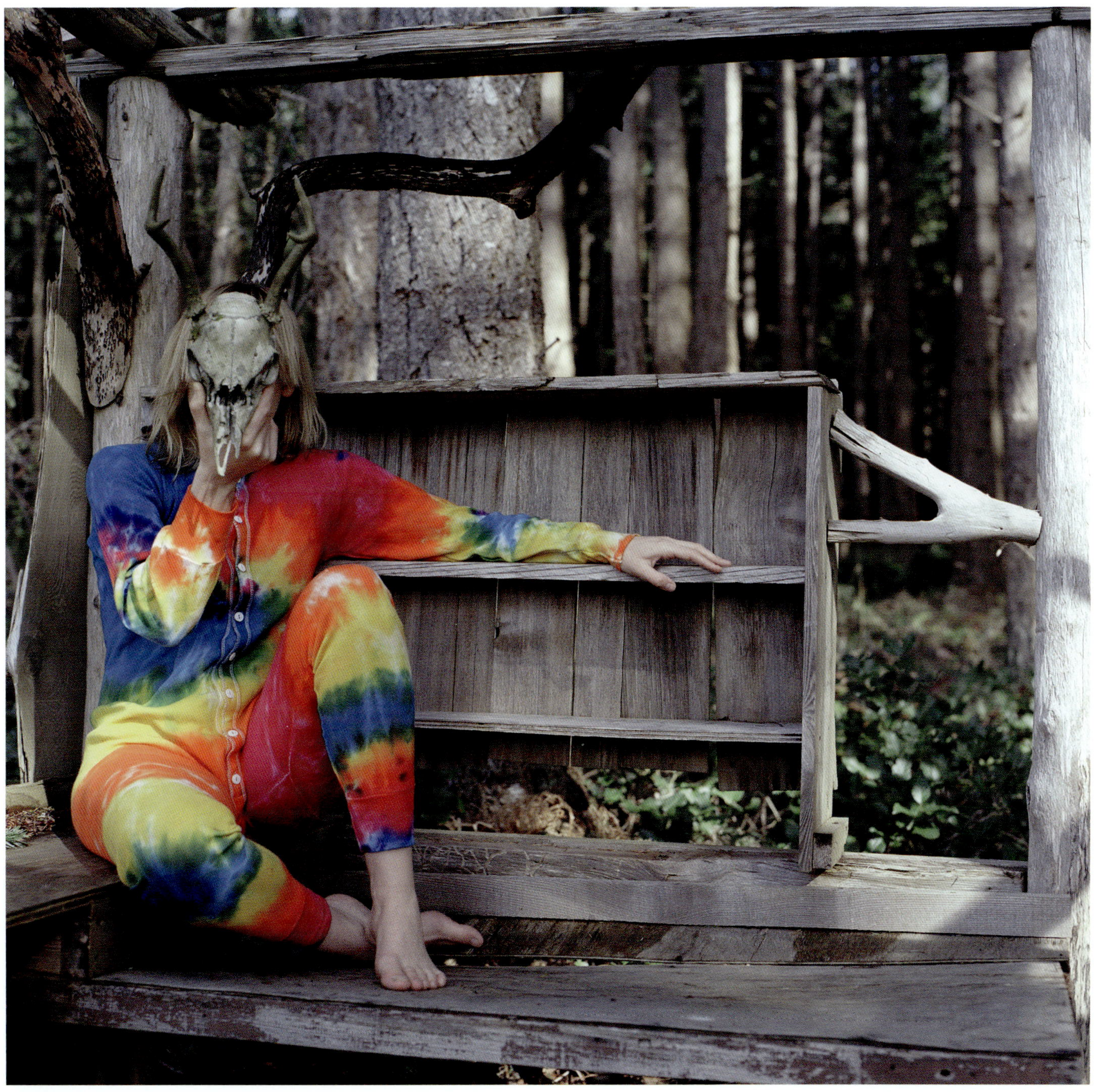

Sycorax

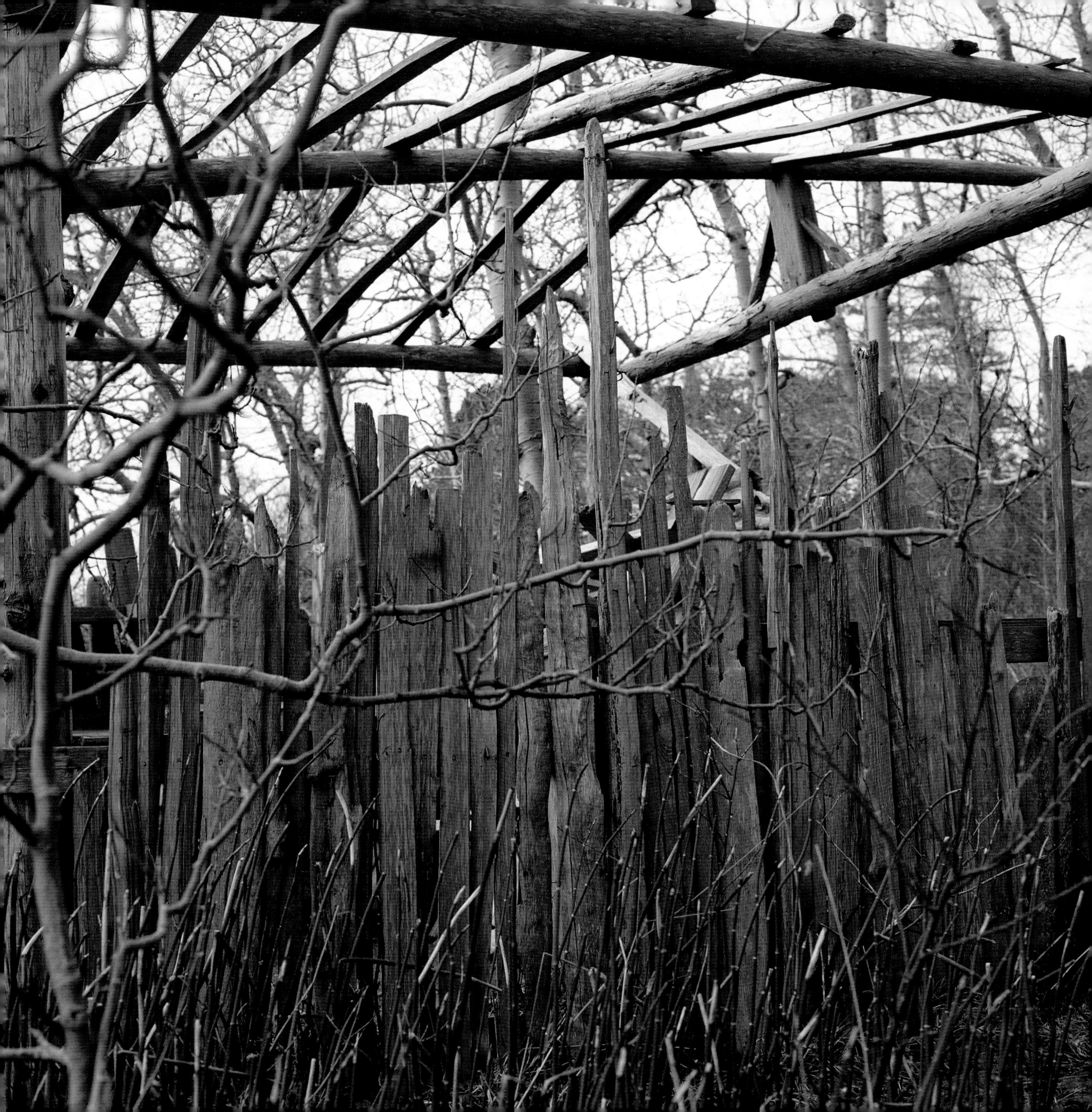

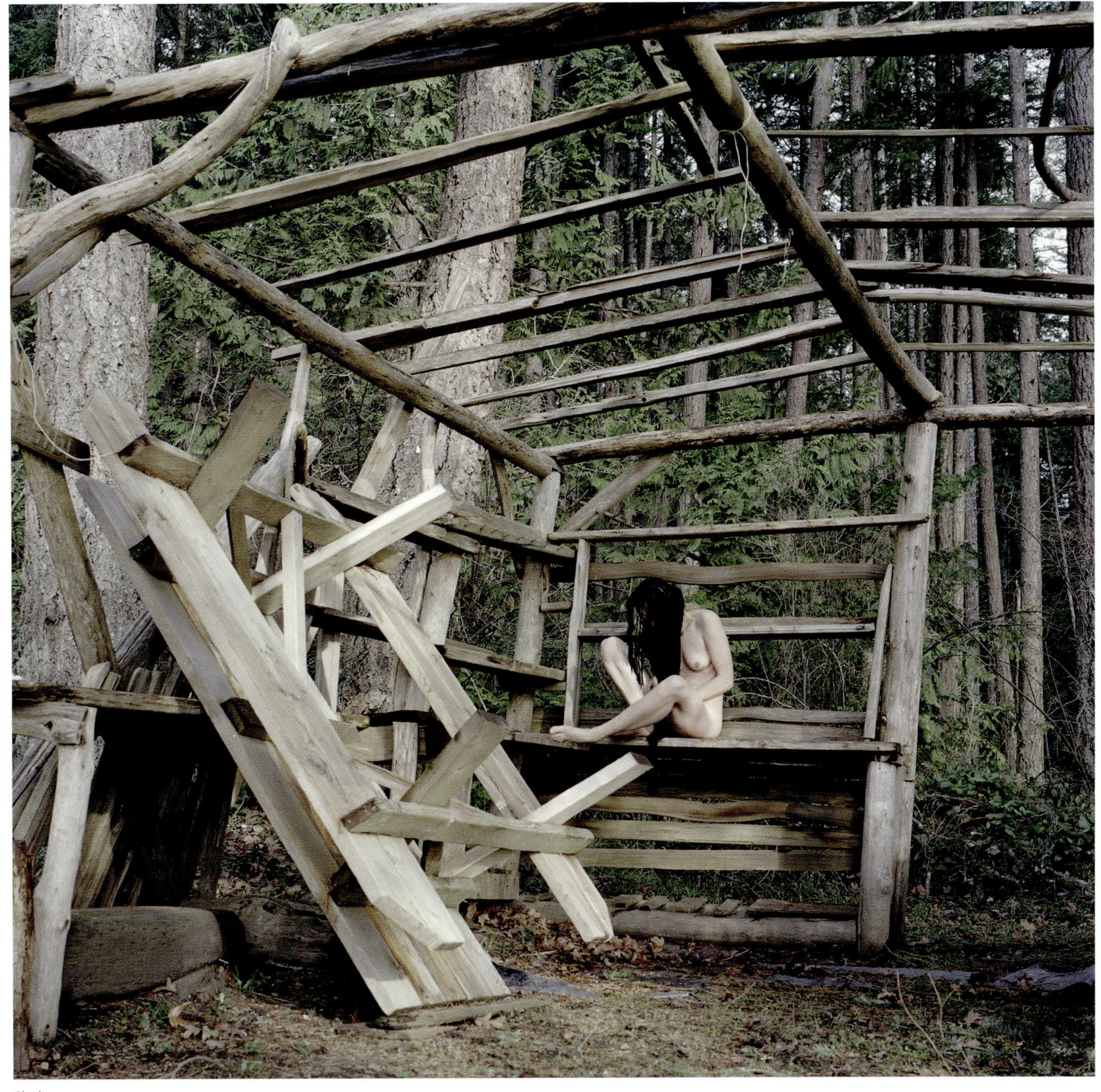

Shelter

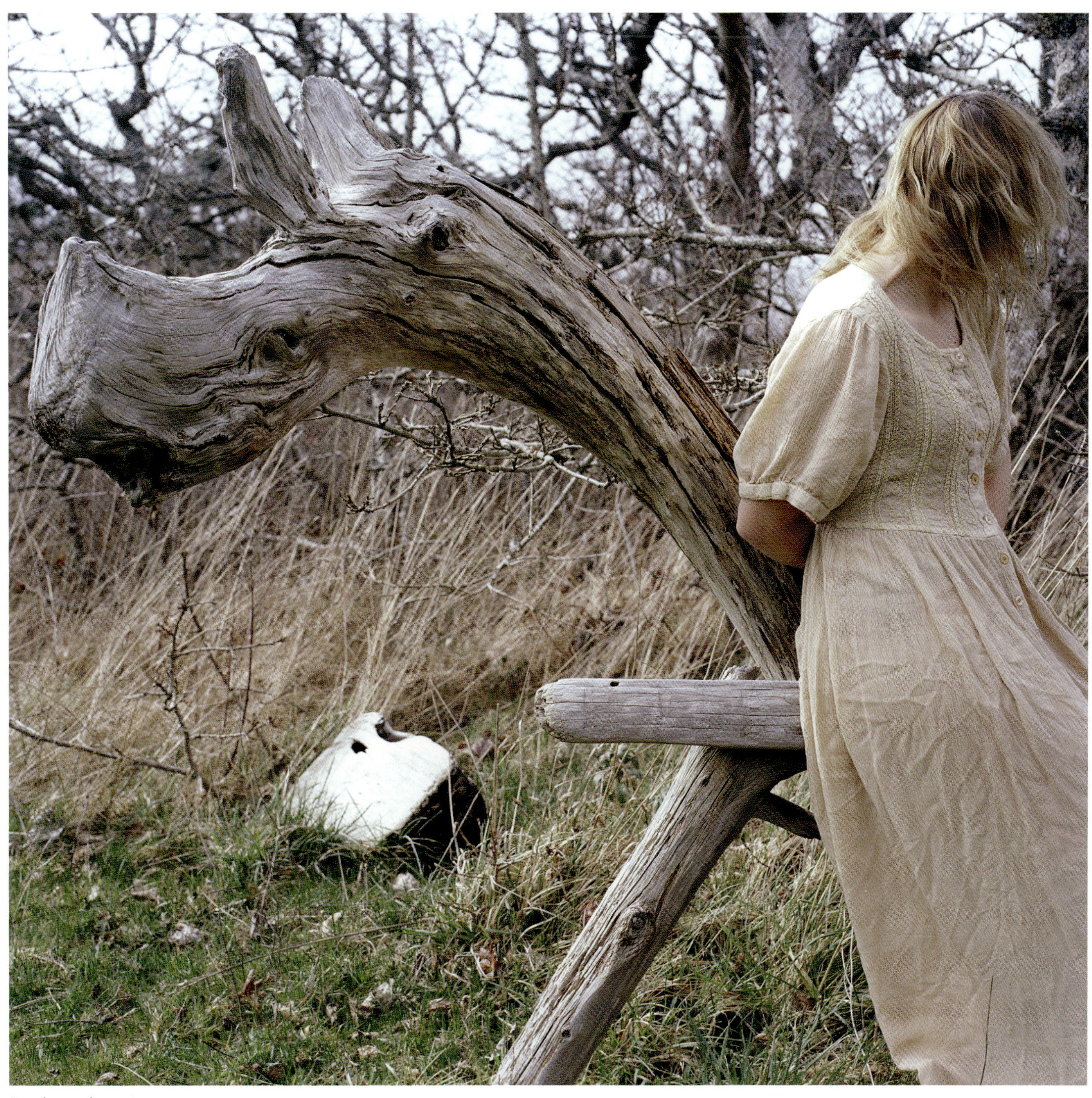
Raggle-taggle

No Horses ▶

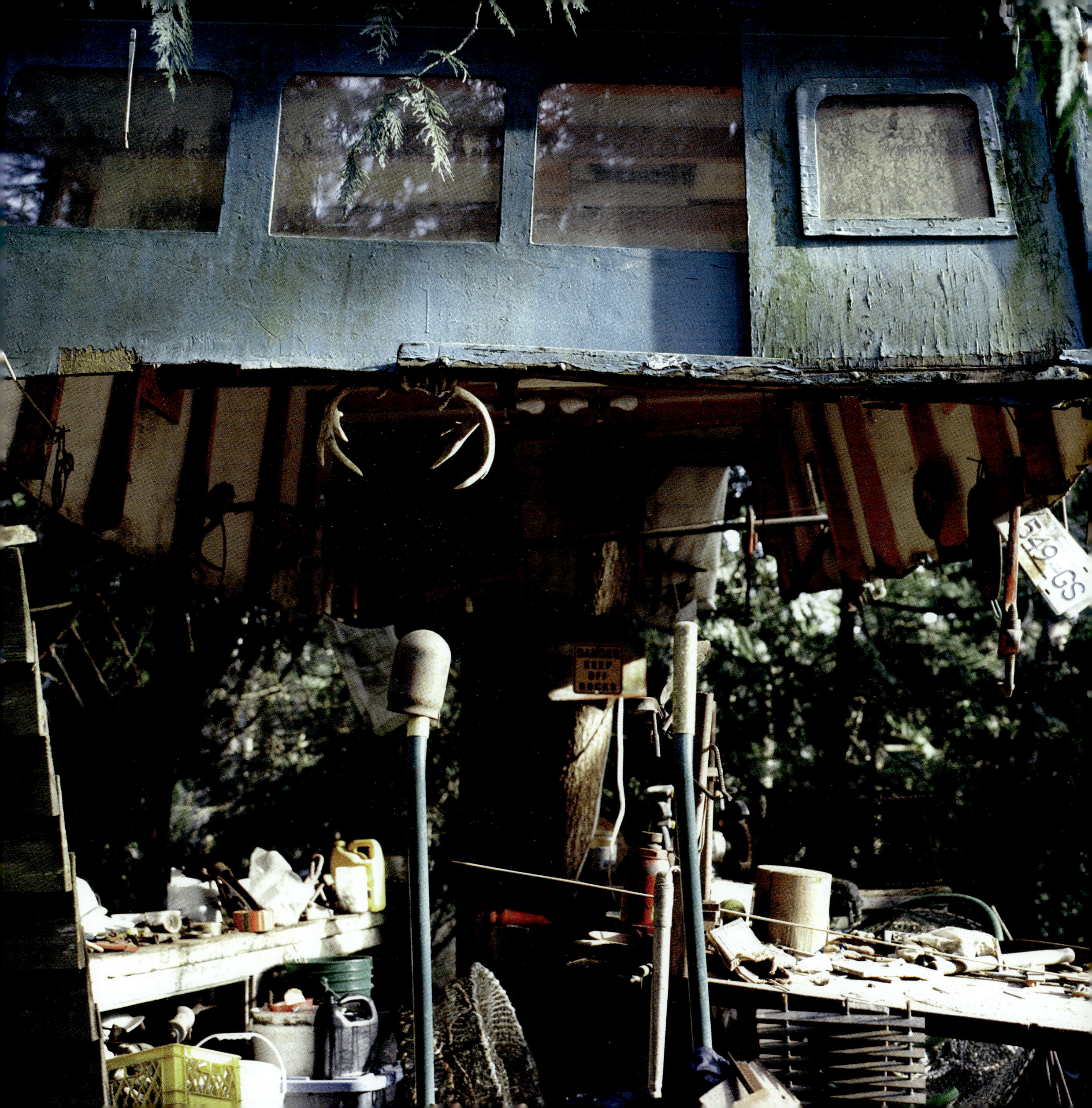

DANGER
KEEP
OFF
ROCKS
540 GS

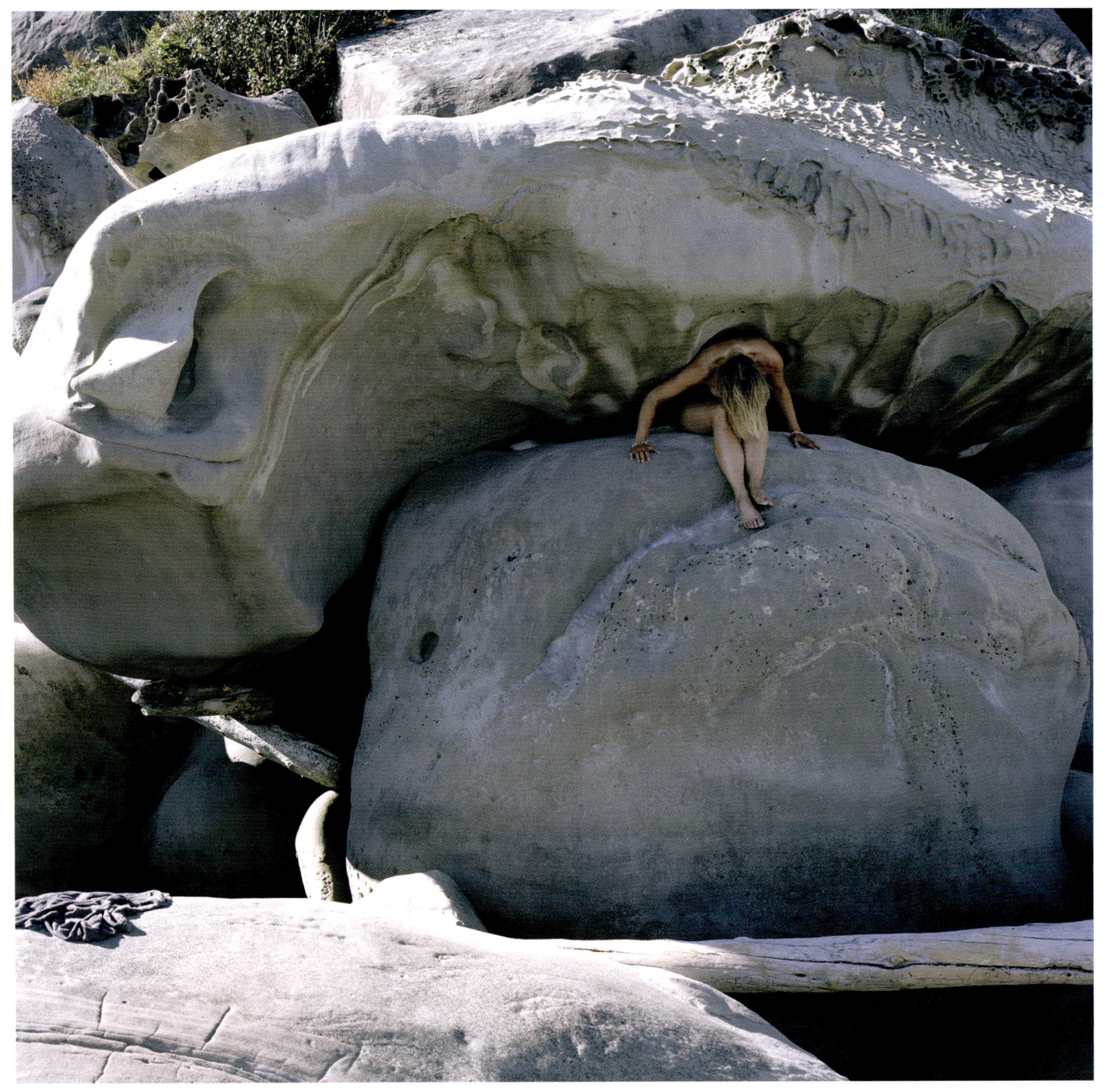

Scales

50

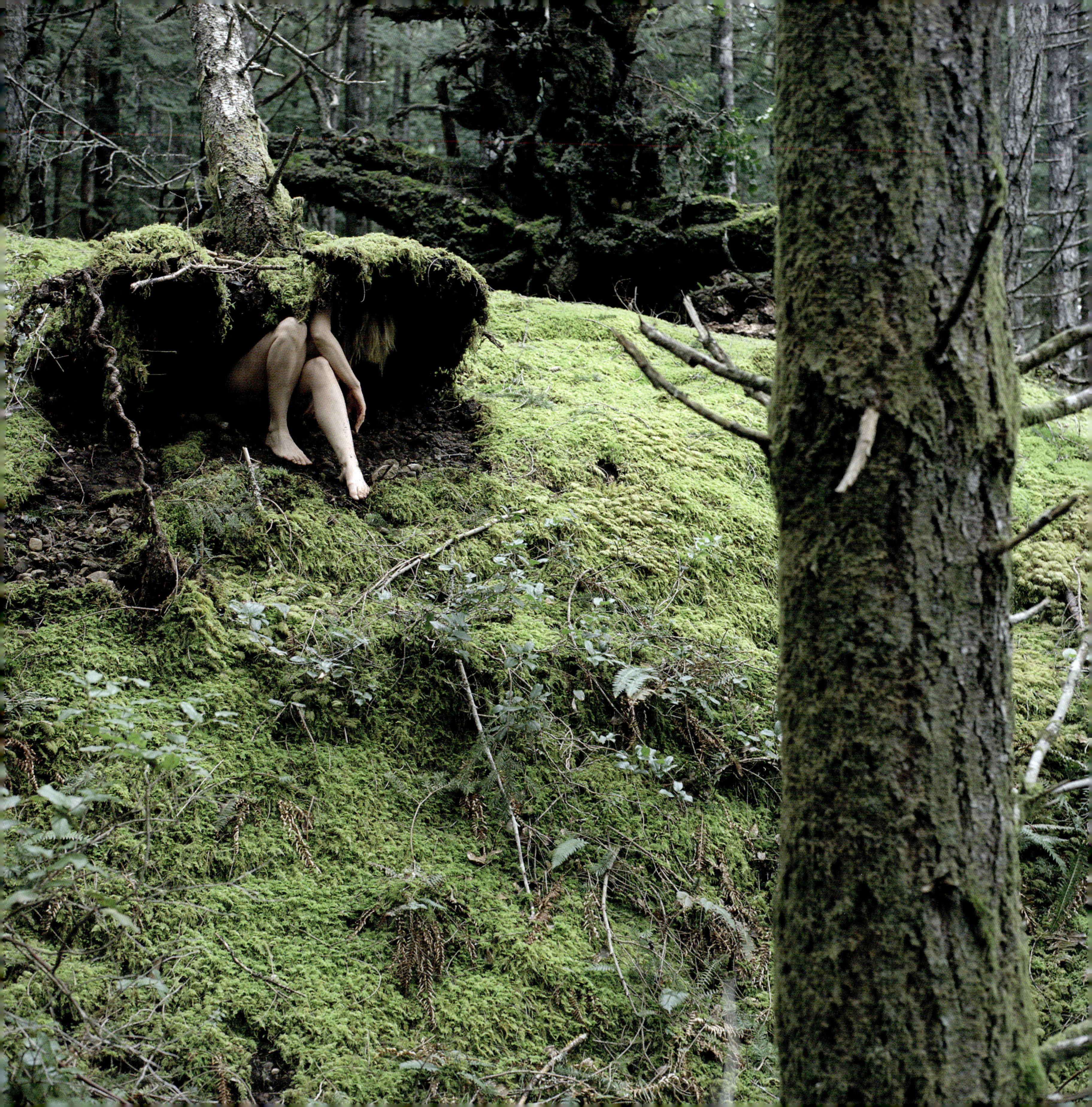

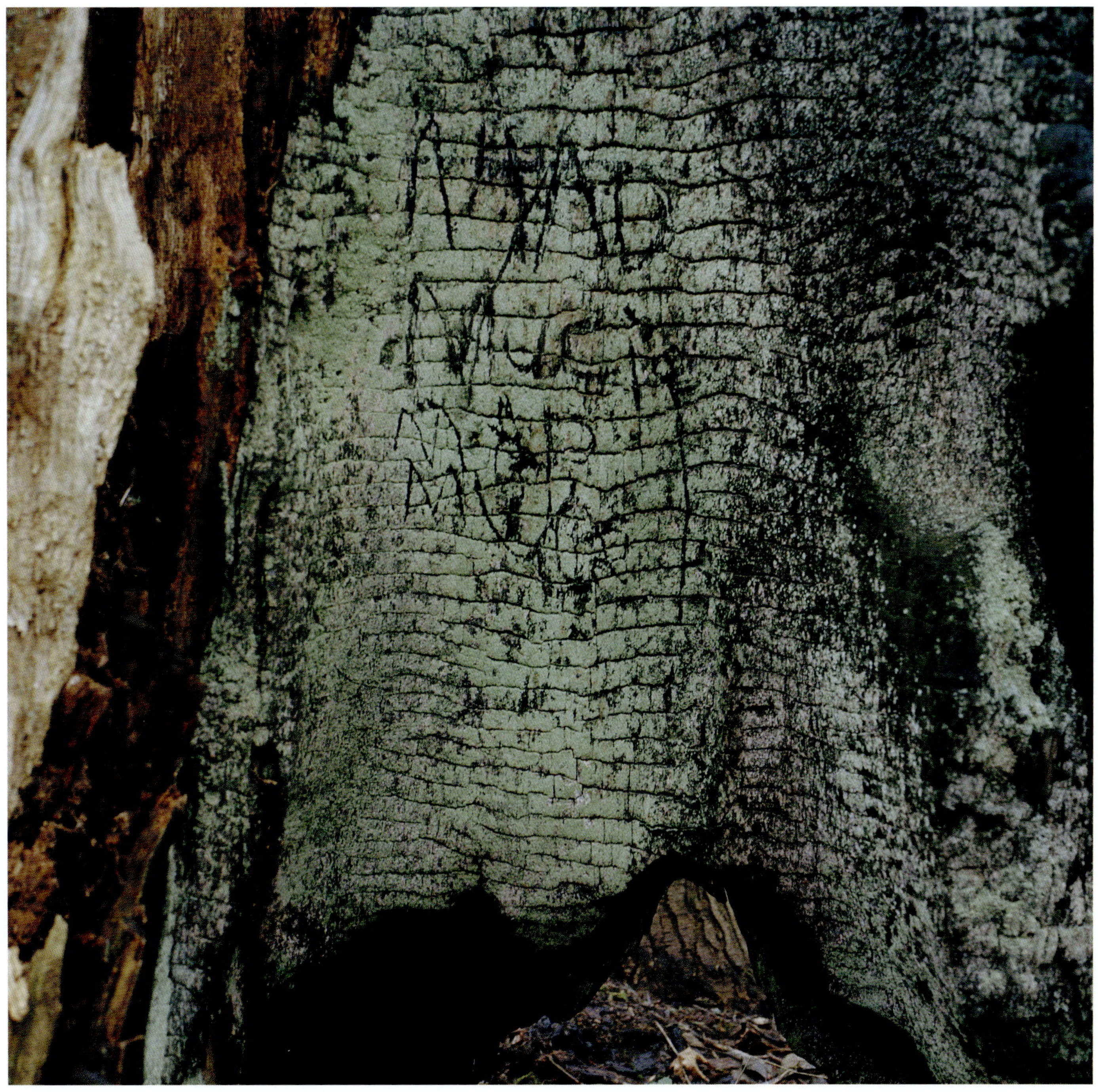

Script

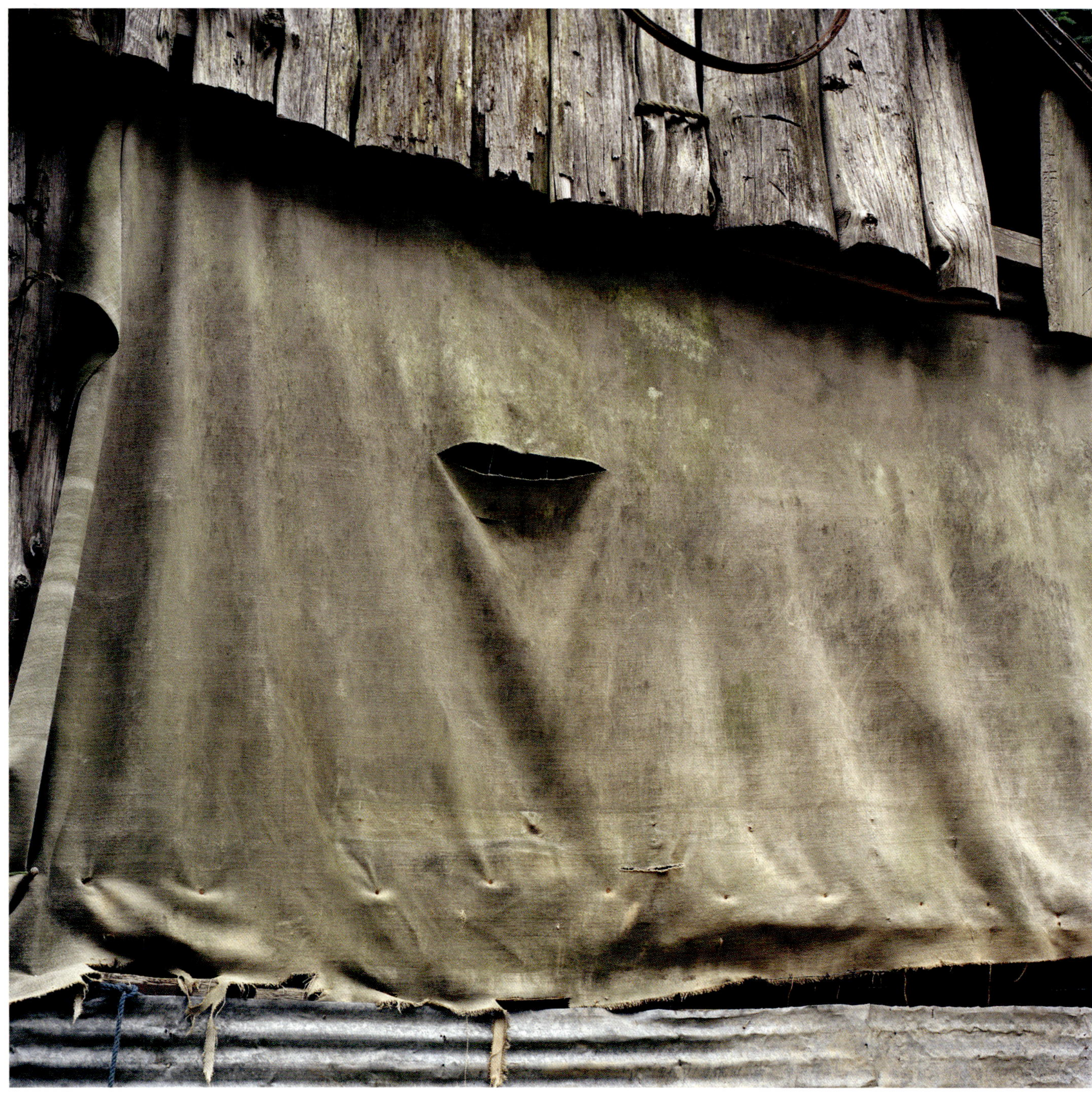

Teatrini

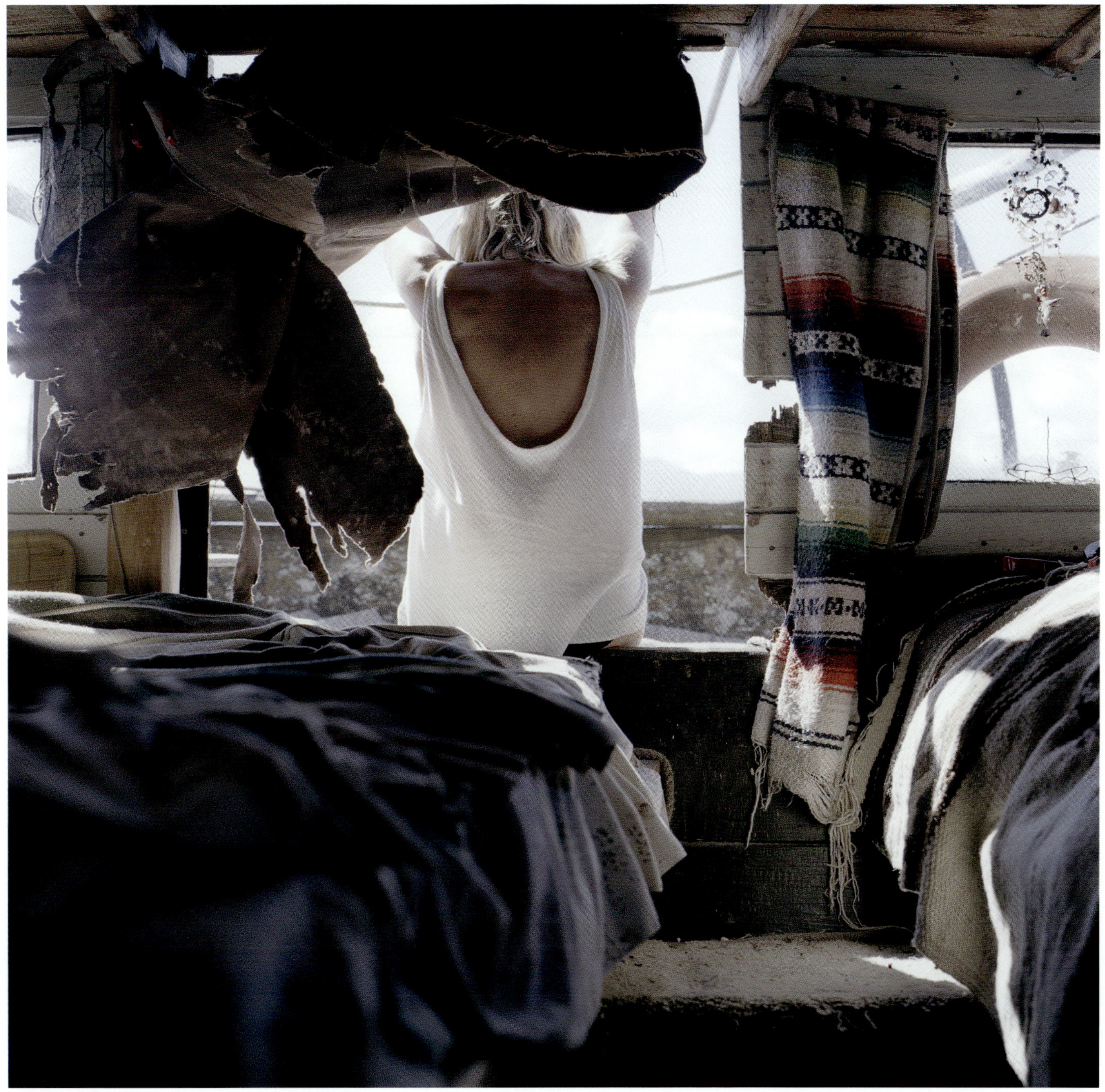

Land Ends

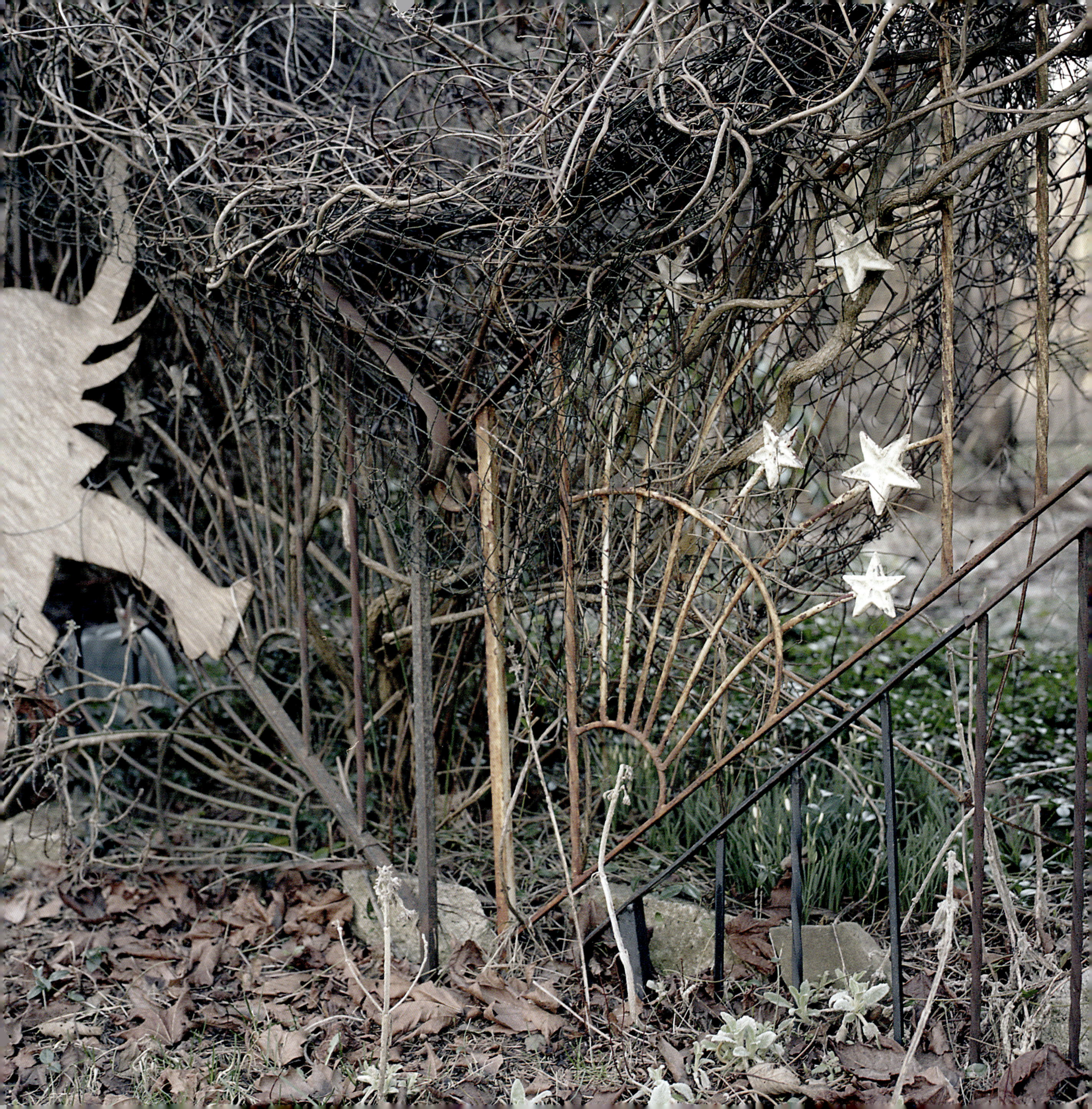

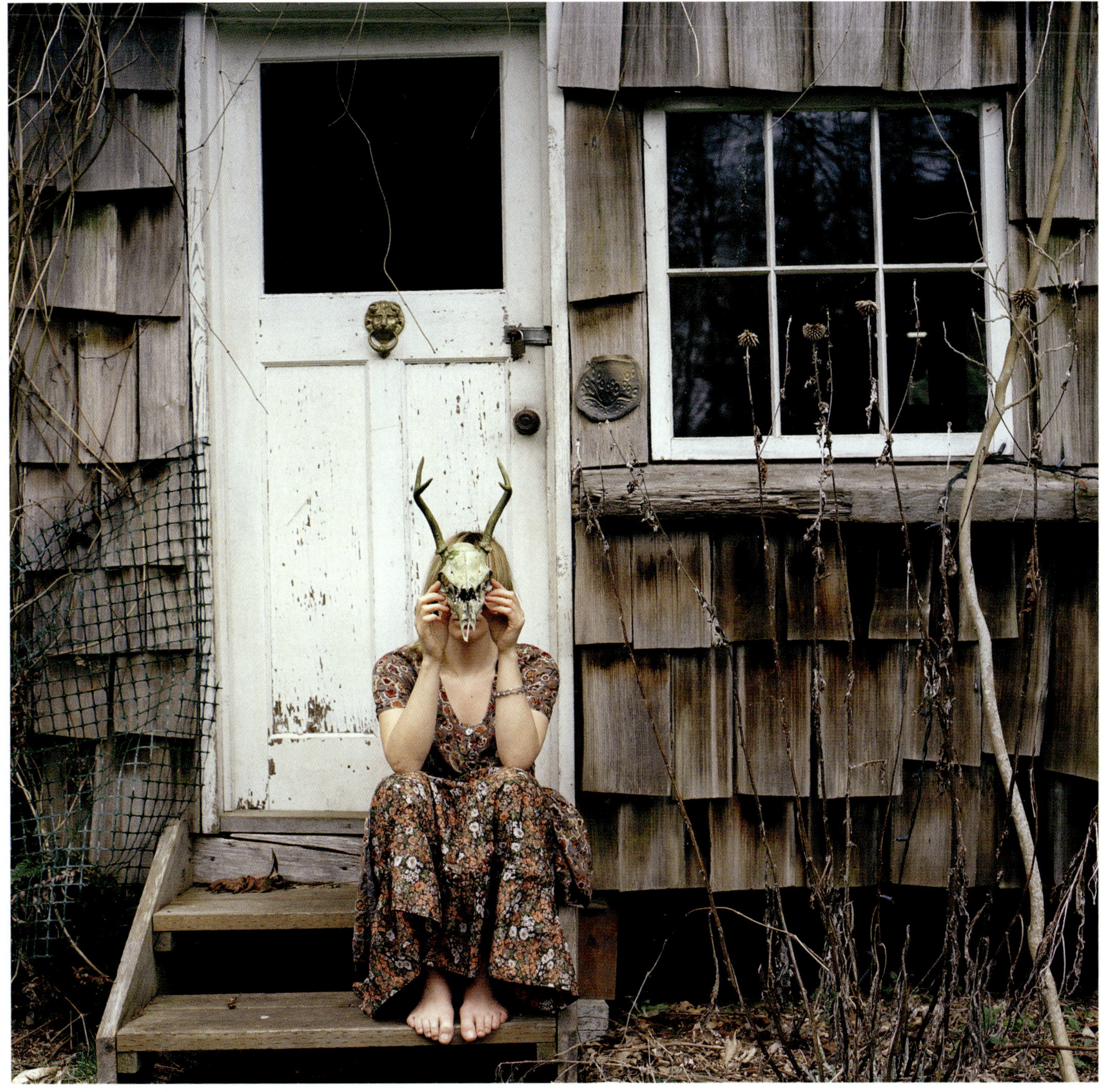

More Reverie

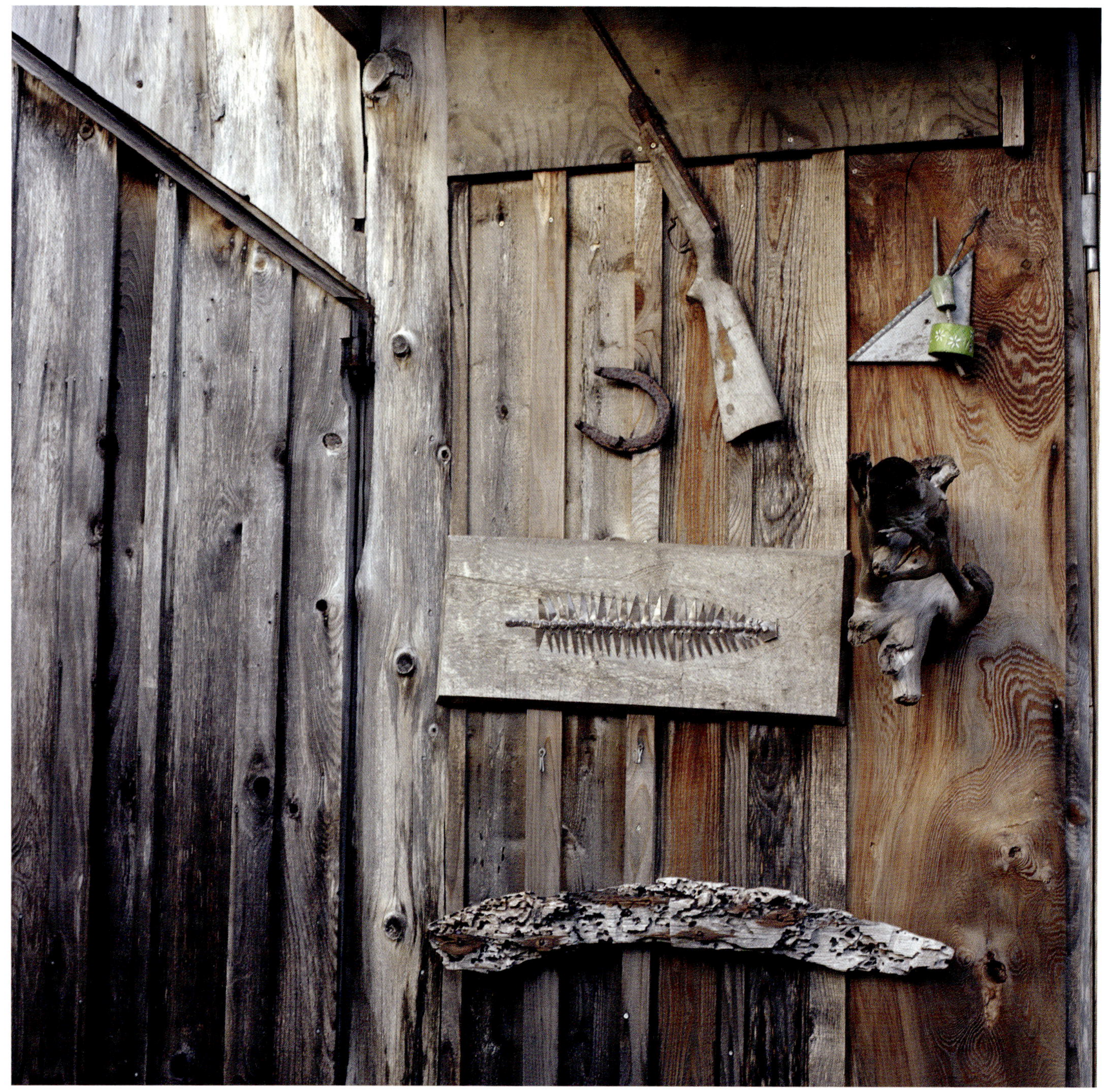

Kingdom

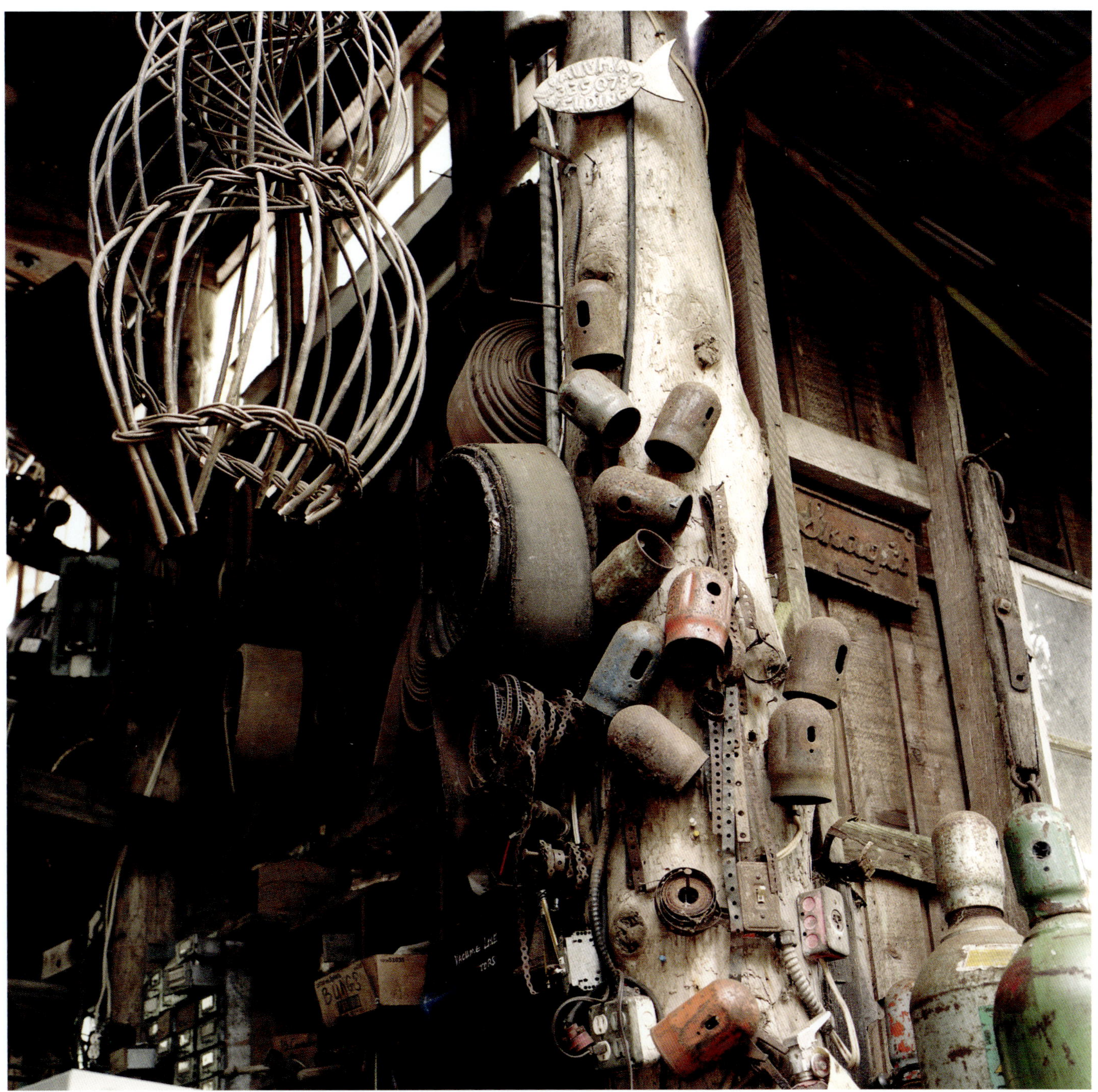

Kit

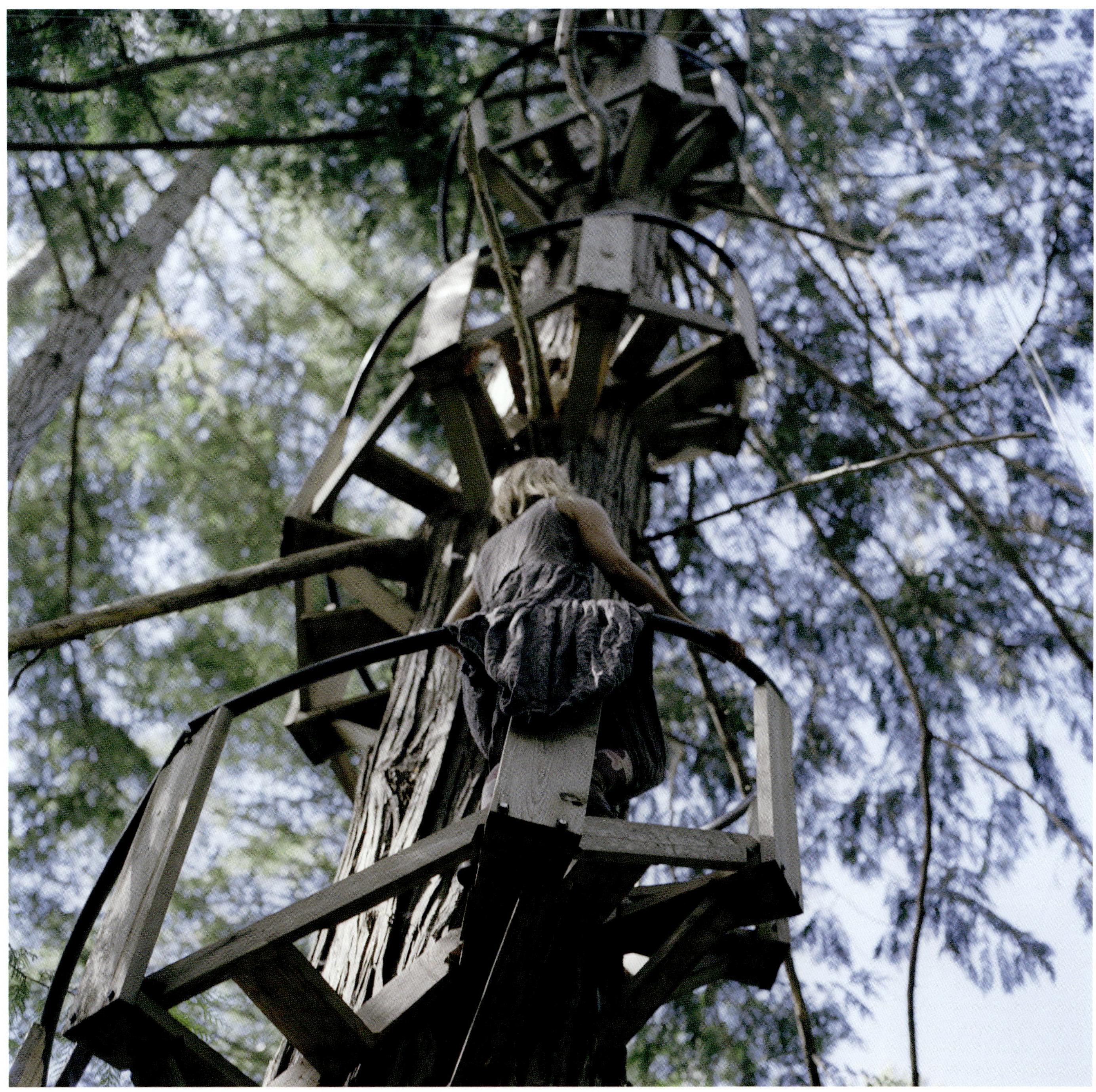

Stairway

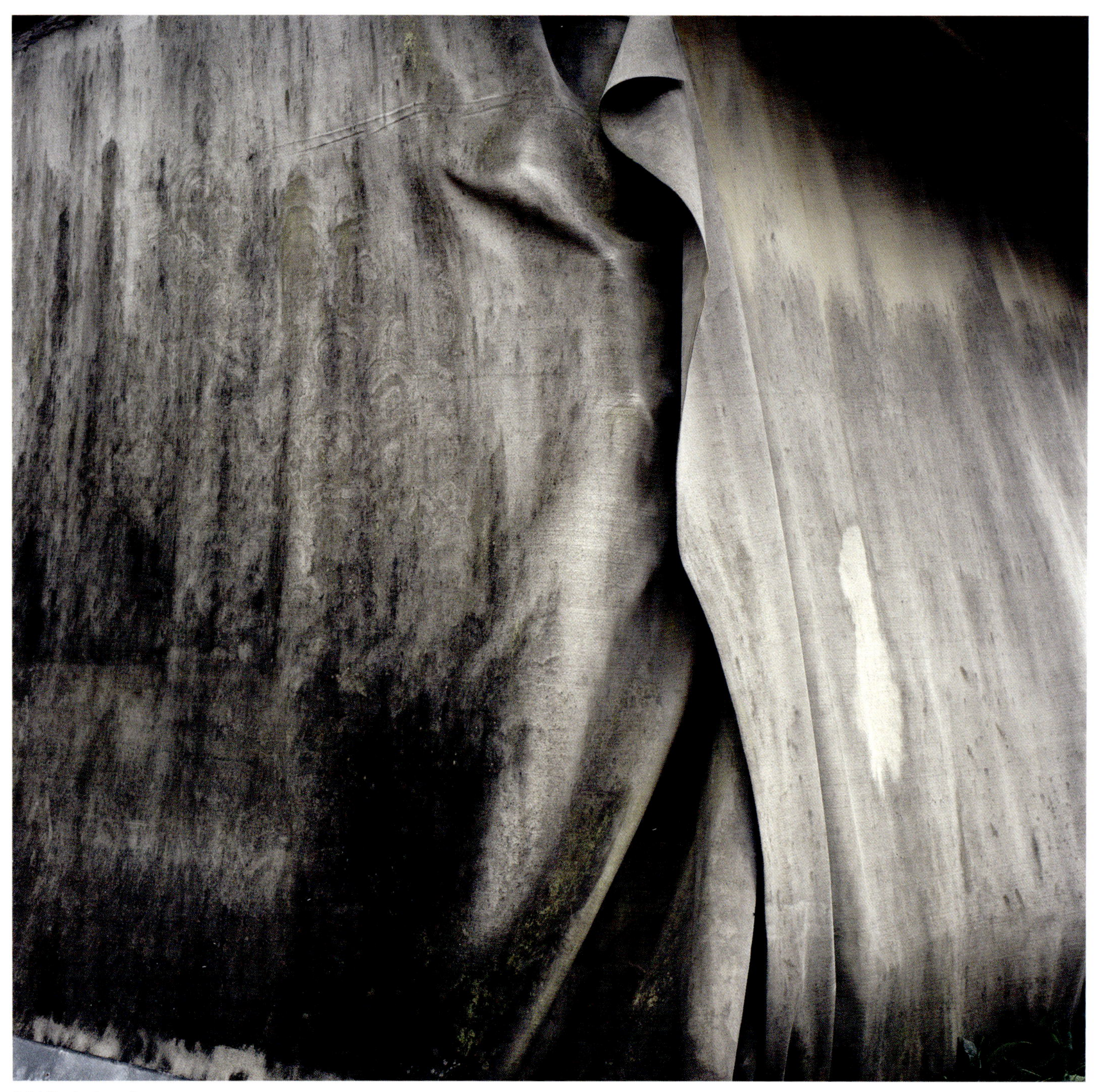

Fold (Dusty-dream)

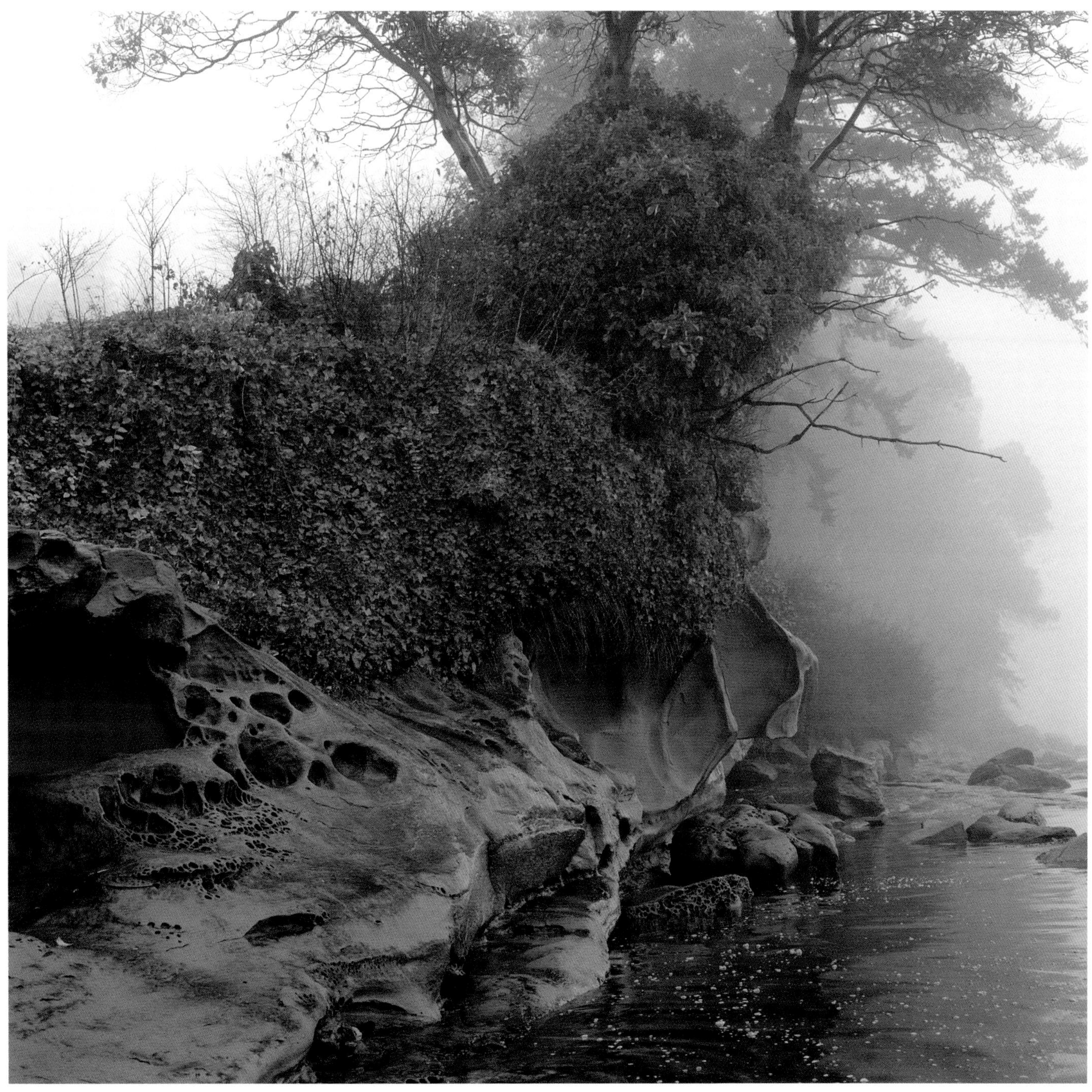

Winter Gone

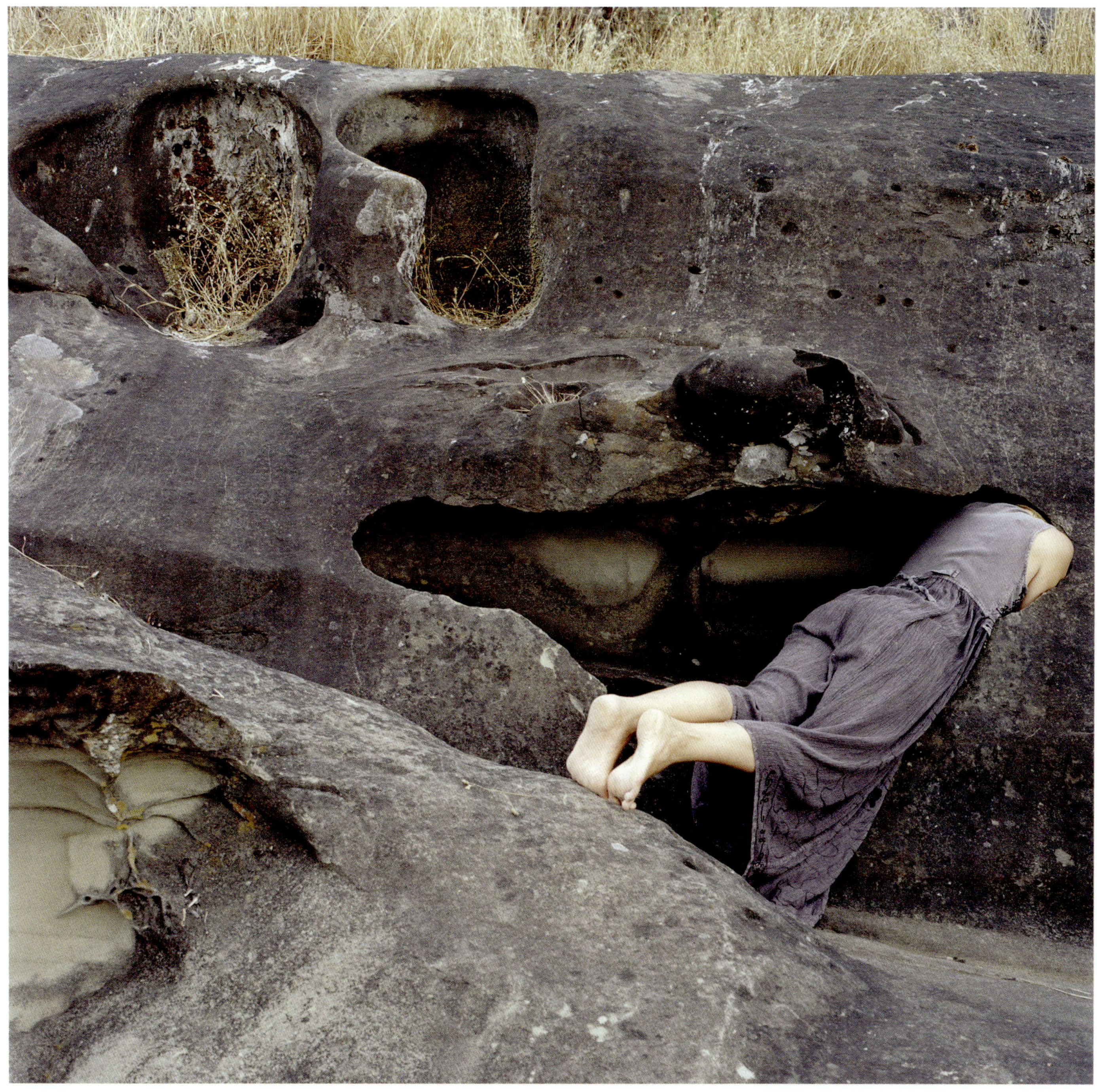

Charm

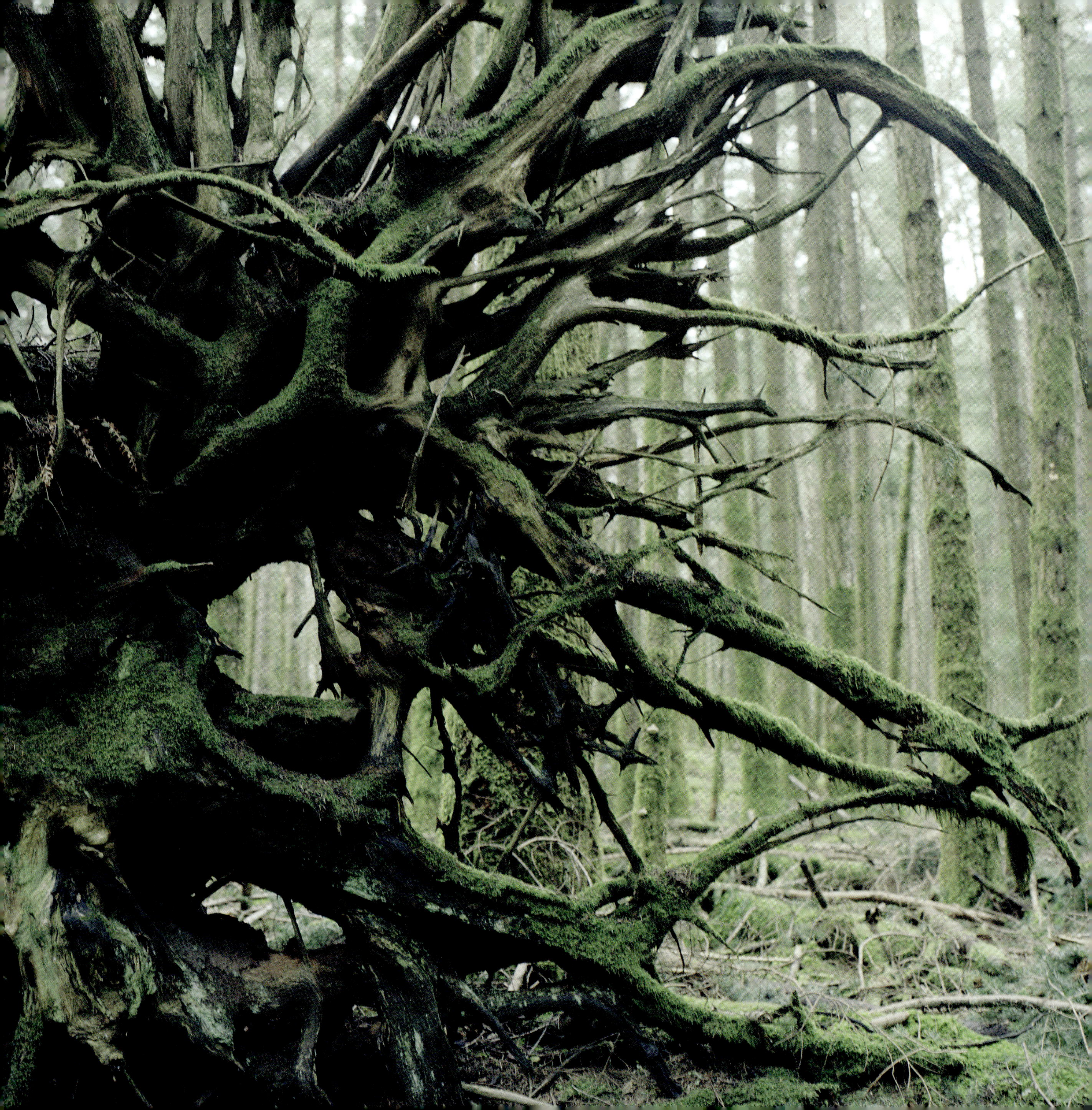

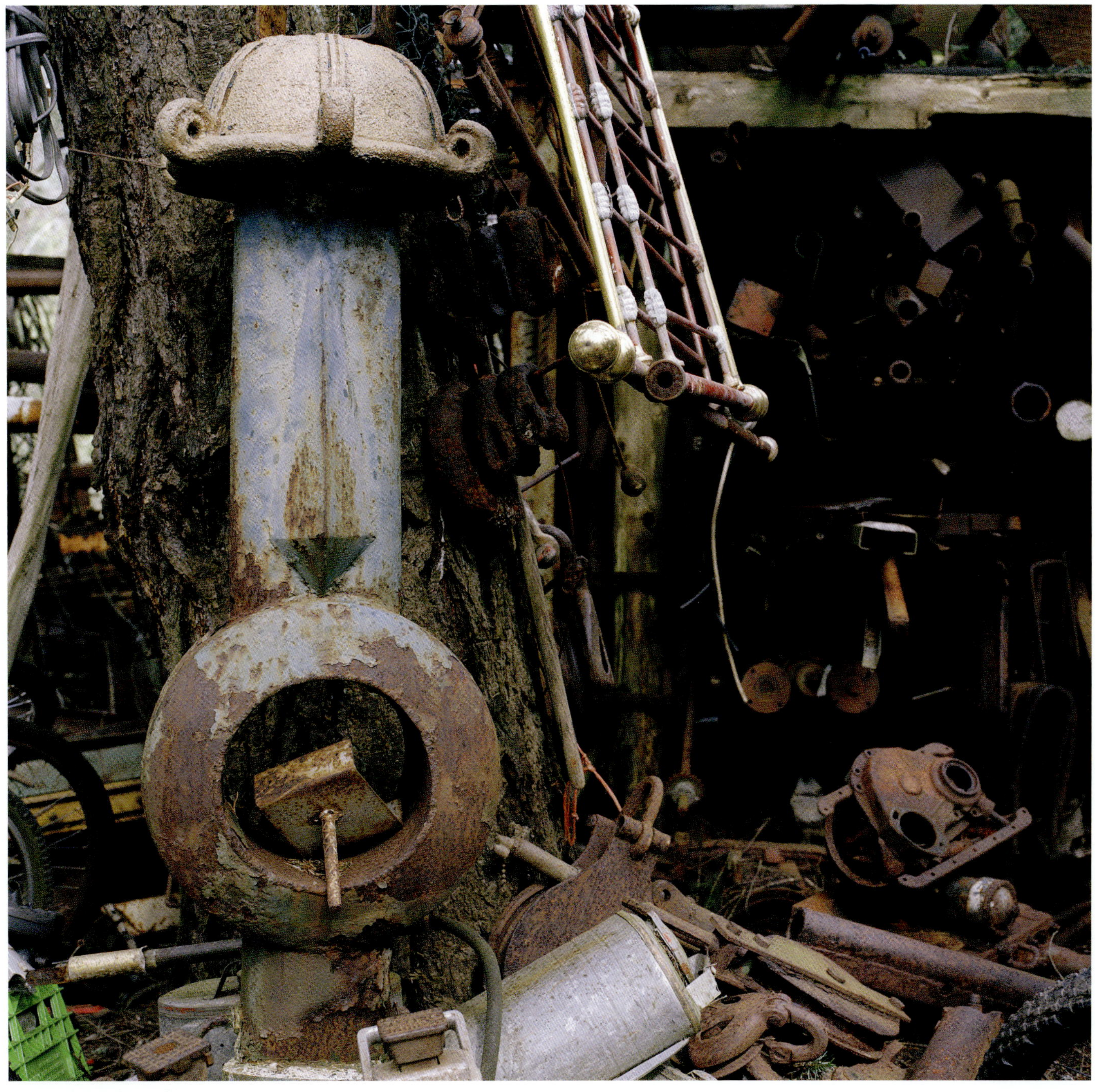

Crown, Ring and Everything

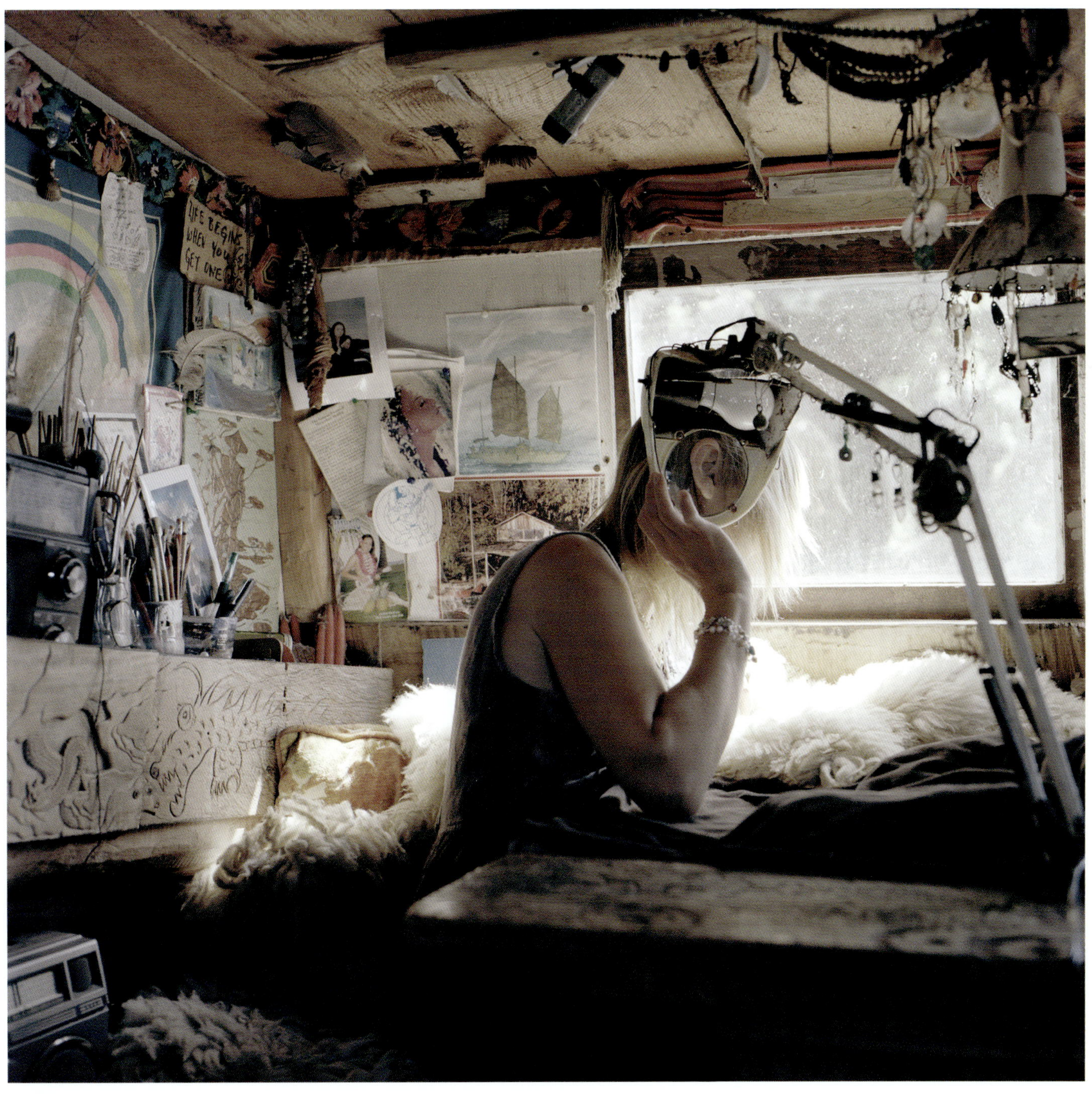

Sweet Airs

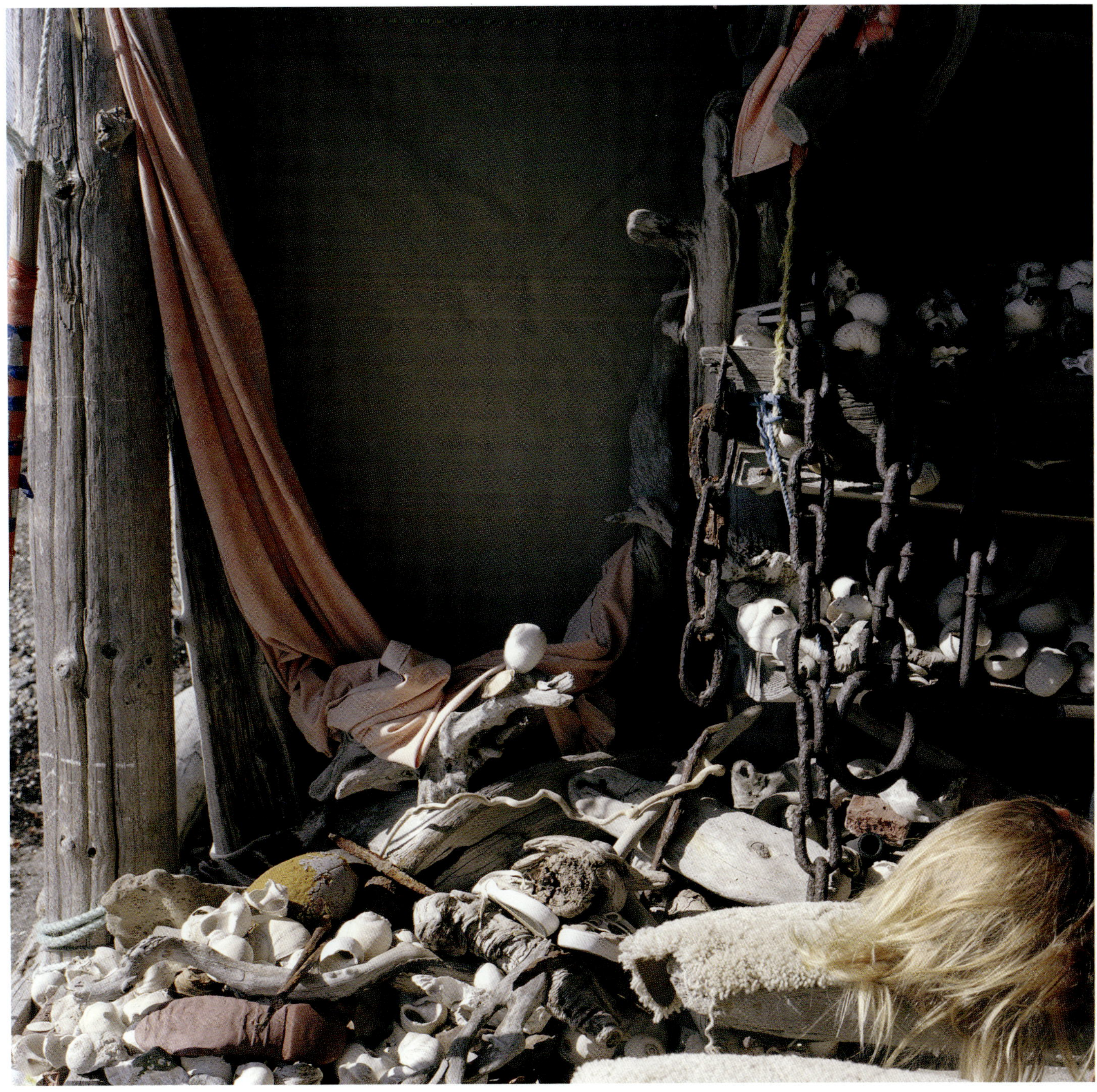

Flotsam

Mark Cousins

RAGS OF TIME

Soon this work commands us to identify the diagram which underpins it. For each photograph repeats the same scene, over and over, again and again. From the side of the photographer, of the camera, of the photograph, we understand that the position of the photographer is invisible except *as* the photograph. She/it captures herself through a time delay. But she is not in a world of portraiture, of using the camera to compose herself. Not only does she delay herself, she hides herself from it or blinds herself to it. So we see her seen by herself where she is not, and we see her not seeing herself, where she is. She hides herself *as* the photograph and she hides herself *in* the photograph. And of course there are some photographs where she does not appear, but where she is gone, eyes and all. Then we start to look for her wondering if she has been buried, or has turned to stone, or become part of a tree or has finally found an exit from photography. She may have vanished and the magic of the time delay may have failed but she certainly isn't absent.

Especially the eyes. In order to avoid being seen she hides her eyes. Which is why we are confused, like Actaeon, by what we see of her body. We have stumbled upon its visibility, we confront its part nakedness. But a body that cannot see itself is always naked, never nude. The spectator is transported to an unusual position— he does not see her, he catches sight of her. This artifice of the entire construction has nonetheless addressed an aspect of daily visual life which photography has neglected—the experience of intrusion, and here something odder, an event of self-intrusion. This has nothing to do with photography's use of scoptophilia or with voyeurism. It is almost the opposite—of coming upon a scene which belongs to someone else, a scene which is private. More like opening the wrong door at the wrong moment and feeling a need to apologize and withdraw.

This photography of not seeing circulates throughout the work. Objects, wood, water, junk, interiors are all visible. But somehow they are not seen. This might answer the question as to why the objects in the photograph are difficult to recall afterwards one by one, although the photograph as an image does stay within the mind. Something of the same seems to be true with light. The photographs are in colour but the colours seem to be gradually drained into the grey of stones and shells and the brown of wood. Colour is dominated by objects which themselves lie between the skeletal, vernacular woodwork and furniture. Or perhaps the light is discouraged in face of the fact that the objects too are blind. For an object to be lit an object must see the light. These objects absorb light but the light returns empty handed. *Still life* has become *nature morte*.

We are left with the remnants of visuality and even these seem to be leaving. The figure who already does not see is herself fleeing or hiding. She has covered herself in clothes which seem borrowed, hand-me-downs from a world where other people have their own clothes. And they seem to have been thrown on at the last moment. The world seems curiously left over. In this case the shutter has clicked too soon or too late. An example of the time delay.

Persilia Caton

SURROUNDED IN SOME WAY

Even within an archipelago, an island is often thought of in terms of isolation and detachment. Hornby Island is one of the Northern Gulf Islands located in the Straight of Georgia on the west coast of British Columbia, Canada. Reached from Vancouver by car, the five-ish hour journey includes crossing two islands and taking three ferries. Like most trips that require an investment of time and money, the reason for "getting away" is pointed.

Common for costal communities in Canada, the initial inhabitants were First Nations people (on Hornby it was the Pentlatch band of the Coast Salish). Pioneers attracted by the island's areas of fertile farmland followed European colonization, both Spanish and British. It was between the 1920s and the 1950s that the island saw an increase in the permanent population and the development of infrastructure: a community hall, school, general store and regular ferry service. The 1960s brought back-to-the-land visionaries—young people seeking an alternative lifestyle (my parents included). The promise was affordable land, self-sustainable living and—there is always a flip side—an escape of sorts.

Situated somewhat outside the rat-race, the motivations for being on Hornby are decidedly emotional, a search for isolation or community, both intertwined with the notions of self-betterment and a nature-based off-the-grid mentality of spatial freedom. Visitors during the summer months, a mix of cabin owners and campers, come for the laidback local "vibe" and the natural beauty of the island: large sandy beaches, wooded mountain biking and hiking trails, grassy meadows, sandstone rock formations. It is common that visitors (and residents alike) stay longer than they intended, or return more often. However, it is the quiet and somber winter months that test the idealized notion of being a full-time resident.

The diverse landscape combined with the unique community create an unnamed allure, perhaps particularly for the artist. The capturing of this intangible characteristic through the depiction of the natural surroundings is one that artists, both local and visiting, are certainly preoccupied with. Melissa Moore first visited Hornby in 1999. Only intending on a single trip, she found herself in the repeat-visitor cycle. *Land Ends*—centred on the human figure in the landscape—was created on Hornby during Moore's long-term visits over a period of five years. Her images are located within the established rhetoric of self-portraiture as a device to speak in non-personal, representational terms. Her work moves swiftly from the sublime to the awkward; utilizing subtle humour she avoids sentimentality. Employing the human form, icons, dress, and the environment she depicts interior spaces—both psychological and architectural. Existing within the images is a constant friction between the island as place, space and landscape. Moore investigates Hornby as a *place* with a specific history and agency; the island as a *space* activated by characters, narratives and actions; and the *landscape* as an aesthetic framing device for constructing a series of photographs. Through the synthesis of this dialectical triad, Moore's series points to the complicated question of "place as simultaneously determined by and determining our being in the world"[1], as explored by philosopher Martin Heidegger. Furthermore, Moore uses textiles and the mimicry of form to explore the human capability for environmental camouflage and social assimilation.

Moore's images construct a representational naming—an uncanny experience—of the place I call "home". I often find myself reconciling the lived experiences with the idyllic perceptions in an effort to put my finger on a truthful and accurate description of Hornby, whether for myself or for the curious. Which returns us to the Heideggerean question, "Do we make places, or do they make us?"[2]

[1] For a discussion on space, place and land-scape in reference to Martin Heidegger, see the collection of essays *Landscape and Power*, ed. W.J.T. Mitchell (Chicago: The University of Chicago Press, 2002).
[2] Ibid., p. xii.

Mark Cousins is Director of History
and Theory at the Architectural Association
School of Architecture, London. He has been
Visiting Professor at Columbia University
and is currently Guest Professor at South
Eastern University, Nanjing, China. He has
written widely on contemporary theory
and spatial relations, and is well known for
his Friday Lectures at the AA.

Douglas Park, U.K. based and internationally
active visual artist, author of literary prose
and critical essays, also exhibition curator,
as well all practices combined.

douglasrpark@googlemail.com
www.myspace.com/douglas_park
www.facebook.com/douglasrpark
+44 7813 271150

Persilia Caton is an arts administrator,
independent curator and writer.
She received her BFA from the Nova Scotia
College of Art and Design, Canada
and has worked for various arts
organizations in Toronto—from the public
gallery to the festival. Caton is currently
based in London, UK and is studying
on the MFA, Curating program
at Goldsmiths, University of London.

Melissa Moore is a London based artist.
She studied at the Manchester Metropolitan
University and has a Master's Degree with
a Distinction in Research from the Royal
College of Art, London. She is an Associate
Lecturer at the University of the Arts
London, and has exhibited and published
internationally.
http://www.melissamoore.info/

Images from the series *Land Ends* were also
featured in *Transcalar Investment Vehicles*,
2012, a film by Hilary Koob-Sassen,
http://hilarykoobsassen.com/

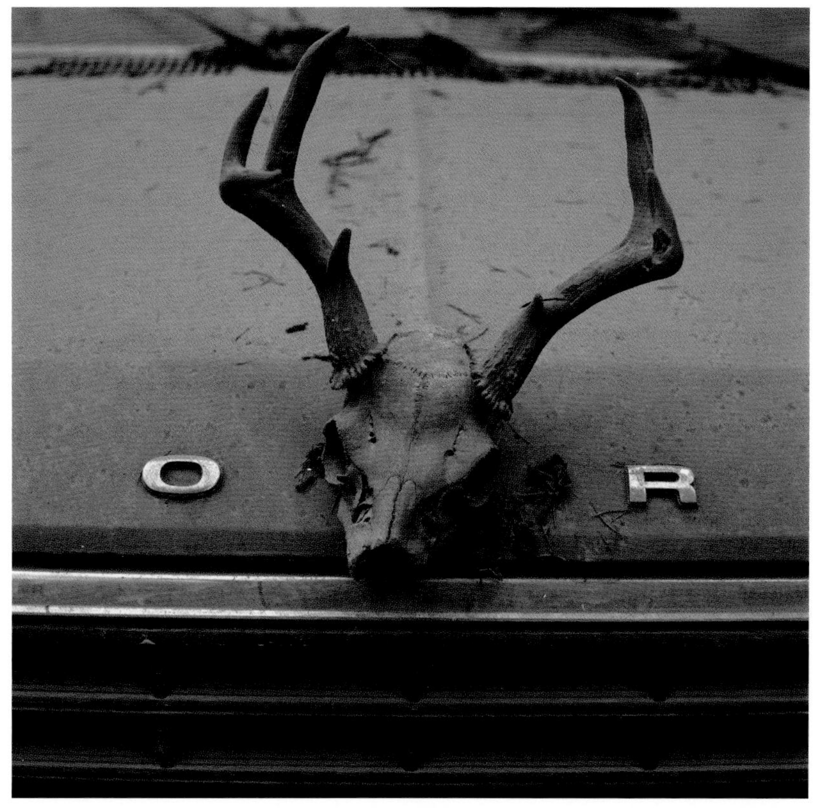

The End